Lonely ⊕ planet

BEST ROAD TRIPS

ROUTE 66

– – – – – – – – →

ESCAPES ON THE OPEN ROAD

Andrew Bender, Cristian Bonetto,
Mark Johanson, Hugh McNaughtan,
Christopher Pitts, Ryan Ver Berkmoes,
Karla Zimmerman

HOW TO USE THIS BOOK

Reviews

In the Destinations section:

All reviews are ordered in our writers' preference, starting with their most preferred option. Additionally:

Sights are arranged geographically and, within this order, by writer preference.

Eating and Sleeping reviews are ordered by price range (budget, midrange, top end) and, within these ranges, by writer preference.

Map Legend

Routes

	Trip Route
	Trip Detour
	Linked Trip
	Walk Route
	Tollway
	Freeway
	Primary
	Secondary
	Tertiary
	Lane
	Unsealed Road
	Plaza/Mall
	Steps
	Tunnel
	Pedestrian Overpass
	Walk Track/Path

Boundaries

– – –	International
- - - -	State/Province
———	Cliff

Hydrography

	River/Creek
	Intermittent River
	Swamp/Mangrove
	Canal
	Water
	Dry/Salt/ Intermittent Lake
	Glacier

Route Markers

97	US National Hwy
5	US Interstate Hwy
44	State Hwy

Trips

1	Trip Numbers
9	Trip Stop
	Walking tour
	Trip Detour

Population

✪	Capital (National)
◉	Capital (State/Province)
●	City/Large Town
●	Town/Village

Areas

	Beach
	Cemetery (Christian)
	Cemetery (Other)
	Park
	Forest
	Reservation
	Urban Area
	Sportsground

Transport

✈	Airport
Ⓑ	BART station
Ⓣ	Boston T station
⊕	Cable Car/ Funicular
Ⓜ	Metro/Muni station
Ⓟ	Parking
Ⓢ	Subway station
⊕	Train/Railway
⊕	Tram
Ⓤ	Underground station

Note: Not all symbols displayed above appear on the maps in this book

Symbols In This Book

✓	Top Tips	🍷	Food & Drink
🔗	Link Your Trips	🌳	Outdoors
💬	Tips from Locals	📷	Essential Photo
↪	Trip Detour	🏃	Walking Tour
📖	History & Culture	✗	Eating
👪	Family		

👁	Sights	🛏	Sleeping
🏖	Beaches	✗	Eating
🏃	Activities	🍷	Drinking
🎓	Courses	☆	Entertainment
☞	Tours	🛍	Shopping
✹	Festivals & Events	ⓘ	Information & Transport

These symbols and abbreviations give vital information for each listing:

☎	Telephone number	🐾	Pet-friendly
⊙	Opening hours	🚌	Bus
Ⓟ	Parking	⛴	Ferry
⊝	Nonsmoking	🚊	Tram
❄	Air-conditioning	🚆	Train
@	Internet access	apt	apartments
🛜	Wi-fi access	d	double rooms
🏊	Swimming pool	dm	dorm beds
🥗	Vegetarian selection	q	quad rooms
📖	English-language menu	r	rooms
		s	single rooms
👪	Family-friendly	ste	suites
		tr	triple rooms
		tw	twin rooms

CONTENTS

ROAD TRIPS

DESTINATIONS

USA DRIVING GUIDE 120

COVID-19

We have re-checked every business in this book before publication to ensure that it is still open after the COVID-19 outbreak. However, the economic and social impacts of COVID-19 will continue to be felt long after the outbreak has been contained, and many businesses, services and events referenced in this guide may experience ongoing restrictions. Some businesses may be temporarily closed, have changed their opening hours and services, or require bookings; some will unfortunately have closed their doors permanently. We suggest you check with venues before visiting for the latest information.

WELCOME TO
ROUTE 66

For a classic American road trip, nothing beats good ol' Route 66. Nicknamed the nation's 'Mother Road' by novelist John Steinbeck, this string of small-town main streets and country byways first connected big-shouldered Chicago with the waving palm trees of Los Angeles in 1926.

Whether you seek to explore retro Americana or simply want to experience big horizons and captivating scenery far from the madding crowd, Route 66 will take you there. Mingle with farmers in Illinois and country-and-western stars in Missouri; hear the legends of cowboys and Indians in Oklahoma; visit Native American tribal nations and contemporary pueblos across the Southwest, all the while discovering the traditions of the USA's indigenous peoples. Continue by following the trails of miners and desperados deep into the Old West. At road's end lie the Pacific beaches of sun-kissed Southern California.

Route 66, Mojave Desert (p36), California
NICK FOX / SHUTTERSTOCK ©

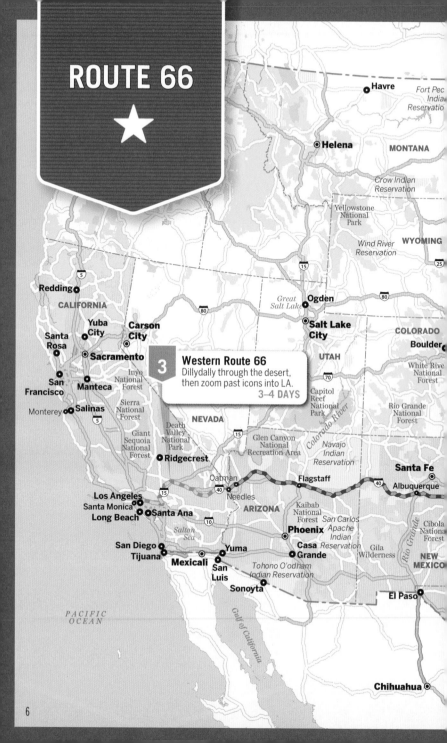

ROUTE 66

★

Helena

Havre
Fort Pec
India
Reservatio

MONTANA

Crow Indian
Reservation

Yellowstone
National
Park

Wind River
Reservation

WYOMING

Redding

CALIFORNIA

Santa
Rosa

Yuba
City

Carson
City

Sacramento

San
Francisco

Manteca

Monterey

Salinas

Great
Salt Lake

Ogden

Salt Lake
City

UTAH

COLORADO

Boulder

White Rive
National
Forest

Inyo
National
Forest

Sierra
National
Forest

Giant
Sequoia
National
Forest

Death
Valley
National
Park

Ridgecrest

NEVADA

Capitol
Reef
National
Park

Rio Grande
National
Forest

3 Western Route 66
Dillydally through the desert,
then zoom past icons into LA.
3–4 DAYS

Glen Canyon
National
Recreation Area

Navajo
Indian
Reservation

Santa Fe

Oatman

Flagstaff

Albuquerque

Los Angeles

Santa Monica

Long Beach

Needles

ARIZONA

Kaibab
National
Forest

San Carlos
Apache
Indian
Reservation

Cibola
Nationa
Forest

Santa Ana

Salton
Sea

Phoenix

Gila
Wilderness

NEW
MEXICO

San Diego

Tijuana

Mexicali

Yuma

San
Luis

Casa
Grande

Tohono O'odham
Indian Reservation

Sonoyta

El Paso

PACIFIC
OCEAN

Chihuahua

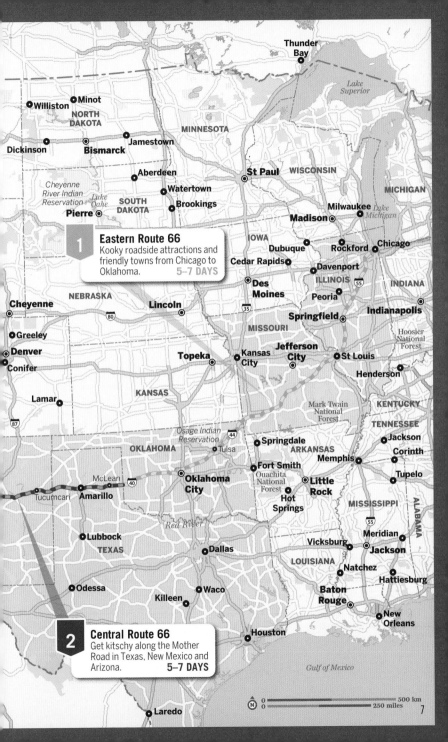

Thunder
Bay

Lake Superior

Williston Minot
NORTH
DAKOTA

Dickinson Bismarck Jamestown

MINNESOTA

Aberdeen
St Paul WISCONSIN

Cheyenne River Indian Reservation *Lake Oahe* Watertown
SOUTH
DAKOTA Brookings MICHIGAN

Pierre Milwaukee *Lake Michigan*

Madison

1 **Eastern Route 66**
Kooky roadside attractions and friendly towns from Chicago to Oklahoma. **5–7 DAYS**

IOWA

Dubuque Rockford Chicago

Cedar Rapids Davenport

Des
Moines ILLINOIS 55 INDIANA

NEBRASKA

Cheyenne Lincoln Peoria

80 35

Greeley Springfield Indianapolis

MISSOURI

Denver
Conifer Topeka Kansas
City Jefferson
City St Louis *Hoosier National Forest*

Henderson

KANSAS *Mark Twain National Forest* KENTUCKY

Lamar TENNESSEE

87 *Osage Indian Reservation* 44 Springdale Jackson

OKLAHOMA Tulsa ARKANSAS Corinth

Memphis

McLean 40 Oklahoma
City Fort Smith *Ouachita National Forest* Little
Rock Tupelo

Tucumcari Amarillo Hot
Springs MISSISSIPPI

Red River

Lubbock Meridian

TEXAS Dallas Vicksburg Jackson

LOUISIANA 55

Odessa Waco Natchez Hattiesburg

Killeen Baton
Rouge

2 **Central Route 66**
Get kitschy along the Mother Road in Texas, New Mexico and Arizona. **5–7 DAYS**

Houston New
Orleans

Gulf of Mexico

N 0 _____ 500 km
  0 _____ 250 miles

Laredo 7

ROUTE 66
HIGHLIGHTS

★

Tucumcari (above) Home to one of the best-preserved sections of Route 66, including dozens of neon signs that cast a rainbow-colored glow. See it on Trip **2**

Munger Moss Motel, Lebanon (right) This atmospheric motel has welcomed passing travelers for over 40 years. See it on Trip **1**

Santa Monica (left) The end of the line: 2400 miles from its start in Chicago, Route 66 comes to an end in the Los Angeles beachside suburb. See it on Trip **3**

CITY GUIDE

Chicago skyscrapers

CHICAGO

The Windy City will wow you with its cloud-scraping architecture and lakefront beaches. Gawp at the buildings, take in a world-class museum, order a late-night deep-dish pizza and join the local sports fanatics cheering on the football or baseball.

Getting Around

Driving in Chicago is no fun. Traffic snarls not only at rush hours, but also just about every hour in between. Especially for short trips in town, use public transportation to spare yourself the headache. The El (a system of elevated and subway trains) is the main way to get around. Buses are also useful. Buy a day pass for $10 at El stations.

Parking

Meter spots and on-street parking are plentiful in outlying areas, but you can do some serious circling in the Loop, Near North, Lincoln Park and Lake View to find a spot. Per-hour costs range from $2 in outlying areas to $6.50 in the Loop. In many areas, you do not have to pay between 10pm and 8am. Check the pay box's instructions.

Where to Eat

Chicago's best and brightest chefs cook at downtown's edge on Randolph St, West Loop. Clark St in Andersonville has nouveau Korean, traditional Belgian and Lowcountry crawfish, while Division St, Wicker Park has hip bistros and cafes. Visit Uptown's Argyle St for Thai and Vietnamese noodle houses, and Pilsen's 18th St for Mexican bakeries and barbecue joints.

Where to Stay

Near North and Navy Pier have the most lodgings, but can be crowded and noisy. The Loop has cool boutique hotels, and is convenient to the parks, museums and Theater District. A little removed from downtown's sights, Lincoln Park and the Old Town offer characterful lodgings and fun nightlife.

Useful Websites

Lonely Planet (www.lonely planet.com/chicago) Destination information, hotel bookings, traveler forum and more.

Choose Chicago (www. choosechicago.com) Official tourism site.

Trips through Chicago:

1

Destinations coverage: p44

Hollywood Boulevard, Los Angeles

LOS ANGELES

Loony LA, land of starstruck dreams and Hollywood Tinseltown magic. You may think you know what to expect: celebrity worship, Botoxed beach blondes, endless traffic and earthquakes. But it's also California's most ethnically diverse city, with new immigrants arriving daily, evolving the boundary-breaking global arts, music and food scenes.

Getting Around

Unless time is no factor – or money is extremely tight – you're going to want to spend some time behind the wheel, although this means contending with some of the worst traffic in the country. Avoid rush hour (7am to 9am and 3:30pm to 6pm).

Parking

Parking at motels and cheaper hotels is usually free, while fancier ones charge anywhere from $8 to around $45 for the privilege. Valet parking at nicer restaurants and hotels is commonplace, with rates ranging from $3.50 to $10.

Where to Eat

Beverly Hills and Bel Air offer power-lunch steakhouses and polished bistros. Eat Chinese and Japanese in Downtown, and Mexican in Boyle Heights. Visit Culver City and Mar Vista for gourmet burgers, upscale Southeast Asian, retro Cuban and pizzas. Try Malibu and Pacific Palisades for farm-to-table brunches. West Hollywood and Mid-City have a trendy scene, from northern Thai and vegan Mexican to clever Californian.

Where to Stay

For beach life, escape to Santa Monica or Venice. Long Beach is convenient for Disneyland and Orange County. Party people adore Hollywood; culture vultures, Downtown LA.

Useful Websites

Lonely Planet (www.lonely planet.com/usa/los-angeles) Destination information, hotel bookings, traveler forum and more.

Discover Los Angeles (www. discoverlosangeles.com) Official Convention and Visitors' Bureau website.

LA Curbed (www.la.curbed. com) Delicious bites of history, neighborhood esoterica and celebrity real-estate gossip.

Trips through Los Angeles: 3
Destinations coverage: p96

NEED ^{TO} KNOW

CELL PHONES
Foreign phones that operate on tri- or quad-band frequencies will work in the USA.

INTERNET ACCESS
Most hotels, guesthouses, hostels and motels have wi-fi (usually free). Across the US, most cafes also offer free wi-fi, and some cities have wi-fi-connected parks and plazas.

FUEL
Many gas stations in the USA have fuel pumps with automated credit-card pay screens. Some machines ask for your ZIP code after you swipe your card. For foreign travelers, or those with cards issued outside the US, you'll have to pay inside before fueling up.

RENTAL CARS
Alamo (www.alamo.com)

Car Rental Express (www.carrentalexpress.com)

Simply Hybrid (www.simplyhybrid.com)

Zipcar (www.zipcar.com)

IMPORTANT NUMBERS
American Automobile Association (AAA) ☎877-428-2277

Emergencies ☎911

Highway conditions ☎800-427-7623

Traffic updates ☎511

Climate

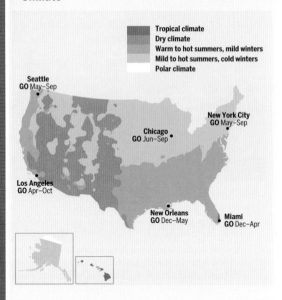

Tropical climate
Dry climate
Warm to hot summers, mild winters
Mild to hot summers, cold winters
Polar climate

Seattle
GO May–Sep

New York City
GO May–Sep

Chicago
GO Jun–Sep

Los Angeles
GO Apr–Oct

New Orleans
GO Dec–May

Miami
GO Dec–Apr

When to Go

High Season (Jun–Aug)
» Warm days across the country, with generally high temperatures.

» Busiest season, with big crowds and higher prices.

» In ski resort areas, January to March is high season.

Shoulder Season (Apr–May & Sep–Oct)
» Milder temperatures and fewer crowds.

» Spring flowers (April) and fiery autumn colors (October) in many parts of the country.

Low Season (Nov–Mar)
» Wintry days, with snowfall in the north, and heavier rains in some regions.

» Lowest prices for accommodations (aside from ski resorts and warmer getaway destinations).

Your Daily Budget

Budget: Less than $150

» Dorm bed: $25–40

» Double room in a budget motel: $45–80

» Lunch from a cafe or food truck: $6–12

» Local bus, subway or train tickets: $2–4

Midrange: $150–250

» Double room in midrange hotel: $100–250

» Popular restaurant dinner for two: $30–60

» Car hire per day: from $30

Top End: More than $250

» Double room in a resort or top-end hotel: from $200

» Dinner in a top restaurant: $60–100

» Concert or theater tickets: $60–200

Eating

Roadside diners Simple places with limited menus.

Taquerias and food stands Outdoor stalls selling tacos, frybread and Sonoran hotdogs.

Farm-to-table In mountain towns and big cities there's a focus on fresh and local.

Vegetarians Choices can be limited in cattle country, but most cafes have options.

Eating price indicators represent price of a main dish:

$ less than $15

$$ $15–25

$$$ more than $25

Sleeping

B&Bs Quaint accommodations that usually include breakfast.

Motels Affordable roadside accommodations, typically outside downtown; popular along Route 66.

Camping Have facilities for tents. Some campgrounds also offer simple cabins.

Sleeping price indicators represent the cost of a double room:

$ less than $100

$$ $100–250

$$$ more than $250

Arriving in the USA

O'Hare International Airport Chicago (ORD)

Rental cars In general, it's more expensive to rent at the airport than downtown.

Train The Blue Line El train ($5) runs 24/7 and departs every 10 minutes or so. The journey to the city center takes 40 minutes.

Shared van service Shuttle vans cost $35.

Taxis A taxi into the city will cost around $50.

Los Angeles International Airport (LAX)

Rental cars Offices and lots are outside the airport, but each company has free shuttles leaving from the lower level.

Buses LAX FlyAway (one way $9.75) runs to Union Station (Downtown), Hollywood, Van Nuys, Westwood Village near UCLA, and Long Beach. For scheduled bus services, catch the free shuttle bus from the airport toward parking lot C. It stops by the LAX City Bus Center hub.

Taxi Taxis are readily available outside the terminals. The flat rate to Downtown LA is $47.

Money

ATMs are widely available. Credit cards are accepted at most hotels, restaurants and shops.

Tipping

Tipping is expected. Standard tips: 15% to 20% in bars and restaurants; $2 to $4 per night for hotel maids; 10% to 15% for taxi drivers.

Opening Hours

Typical normal opening times are as follows:

Banks 8:30am–4:30pm Monday to Thursday, to 5:30pm Friday (and possibly 9am–noon Saturday)

Post offices 9am–5pm Monday to Friday

Stores 9am–6pm Monday to Saturday, noon–5pm Sunday

Supermarkets 8am–8pm, some open 24 hours

Useful Websites

Lonely Planet (www.lonely planet.com/usa) Destination information, inspiration, traveler forum and more.

Roadside America (www. roadsideamerica.com) For all things weird and wacky.

For more, see USA Driving Guide (p120).

Road Trips

1 Eastern Route 66 5–7 Days
Start your trip in the Windy City, then head south through Missouri, Kansas and Oklahoma. (p17)

2 Central Route 66 5–7 Days
Get kitschy along the Mother Road in Texas, New Mexico and Arizona. (p25)

3 Western Route 66 3–4 Days
Meander through the desert, then zoom past retro icons into LA. (p35)

Freeway intersection outside Los Angeles
TIERNEYMJ / SHUTTERSTOCK ©

Eastern Route 66

1

Argue if you want, but we all know that 66's goofiest roadside attractions, friendliest small towns and best pie-filled diners pop up on the eastern swath, from Chicago to western Oklahoma.

TRIP HIGHLIGHTS

155 miles

Atlanta
Pie and a hot
dog-loving lumberjack

START
Chicago

3

Springfield

450 miles

Lebanon
Ozark neon, root beer
and bowling

St Louis

7

Tulsa

FINISH
12
Oklahoma City

994 miles

Clinton
Route 66 Museum
Multimedia trove tells
the road's story

5–7 DAYS
1050 MILES /
1690KM

GREAT FOR...

BEST TIME TO GO

May to September
for extended opening
hours at attractions.

ESSENTIAL PHOTO

The Gemini Giant, a
fiberglass spaceman
in Wilmington, IL.

BEST TWO DAYS

Oklahoma has
more miles of the
original alignment
than anywhere, plus
cowboys and chicken-
fried steak.

Left The Gemini Giant (p19), Wilmington

17

Eastern Route 66

1

It's a lonely road – a ghost road really – that appears for a stretch then disappears, gobbled up by the interstate. You know you've found it again when a 20ft lumberjack holding a hot dog rises up from the roadside, or a sign points you to the 'World's Largest Covered Wagon,' driven by a giant Abe Lincoln. And that's just Illinois – the first of eight states on the nostalgic, kitschy, slowpoke drive west.

❶ Chicago (p44)

Route 66 kicks off in downtown Chicago on Adams St just west of Michigan Ave. Before you snap the obligatory photo with the 'Route 66 Begin' sign (on the south side of Adams, FYI), spend some time exploring the Windy City. Wander through the **Art Institute** (📞312-443-3600; www.artic.edu; 111 S Michigan Ave; adult/child $25/free; ⏰10:30am-5pm Fri-Wed, to 8pm Thu; 🚹; Ⓜ Brown, Orange, Green, Purple, Pink Line to Adams) – literally steps from the Mother Road's

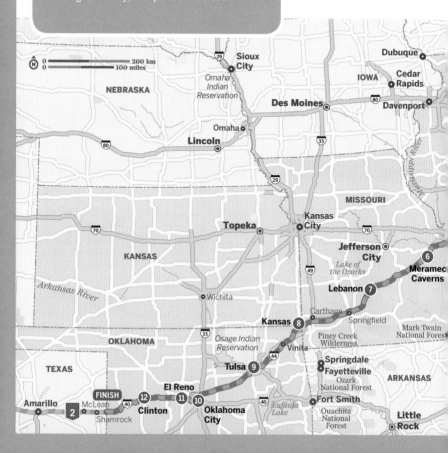

launching point – and ponder Edward Hopper's *Nighthawks* (a diner scene) and Grant Wood's *American Gothic* (a farmer portrait) to set the scene for what you'll see en route. Nearby **Millennium Park** (☑312-742-1168; www.millenniumpark.org; 201 E Randolph St; ⊗6am-11pm; 🚻; Ⓜ Brown, Orange, Green, Purple, Pink Line to Washington/Wabash) is just plain cool, with contemporary public artworks and concerts at lunchtime and many evenings June through August.

LINK YOUR TRIP

2 Central Route 66 (p25)

From the Oklahoma Route 66 Museum, continue west 70 miles to the Texas border. From here Old Route 66 runs immediately south of I-40 through barely changed towns such as Shamrock, with its restored 1930s buildings, including the Tower Station and U-Drop Inn, and minuscule McLean.

The Drive » Stay on Adams St for 1.5 miles until you come to Ogden Ave. Go left, and continue through the suburbs of Cicero and Berwyn. At Harlem Ave, turn left (south) and stay on it briefly until you jump onto Joliet Rd. Soon Joliet Rd joins southbound I-55 (at exit 277), and you're funneled onto the interstate.

- - - - - - - - - - - - - - - -

2 Gemini Giant

Our first stop rises from the cornfields 60 miles south of Chicago. Leave I-55 at exit 241, and follow Hwy 44 south a short distance to Hwy 53, which rolls into the town of Wilmington. Here the **Gemini Giant** (810 E Baltimore St) – a 28ft fiberglass spaceman – stands guard outside the Launching Pad Drive-In. The restaurant is now shuttered, but the humongous green rocket-holding statue remains a quintessential photo op.

The Drive » Get back on I-55. Take exit 154 for Funks Grove, a 19th-century maple-sirup farm (yes, that's sirup with an 'i').

Get on Old Route 66 (a frontage road that parallels the interstate here), and in 10 miles you'll reach Atlanta and its pie-filled cafe. Springfield is 50 miles southwest.

- - - - - - - - - - - - - - - -

TRIP HIGHLIGHT

3 Atlanta

When you hear a collective 'mmm' rising from the cornfields, you'll know that you've reached the throwback hamlet of Atlanta. Pull up a chair at the **Palms Grill Cafe** (☑217-648-2233; www.thepalmsgrillcafe.com; 110 SW Arch St; mains $6-10; ⊗10am-4pm Sun-Wed, to 8pm Thu-Sat), where thick slabs of gooseberry, chocolate cream and other retro pies tempt from the glass case. Then walk across the street to snap a photo with **Tall Paul**, a sky-high statue of Paul Bunyan clutching a hot dog. Continue along Arch St through town to see the old-fashioned murals that cover Atlanta's brick walls.

The Drive » Continue on Old Route 66 (the frontage road) for 10 miles to Lincoln and its sublime statue of Abraham Lincoln helming the world's largest covered wagon. You can try tracing the road for a while longer (it gets tricky), or return to I-55. Springfield is 30 miles onward.

---

❹ Springfield (p60)

Illinois is the Land of Lincoln, according to local license plates, and the best place to get your Honest Abe fix is Springfield, the state capital. Fans of the 16th president get weak-kneed at the holy trio of sights: **Lincoln's Tomb** (☎217-782-2717; www.lincolntomb. org; 1441 Monument Ave; ⏰9am-5pm), the **Lincoln Presidential Library & Museum** (☎217-558-8844; www.illinois.gov/alplm; 212 N 6th St; adult/child $15/6; ⏰9am-5pm;) and the **Lincoln Home** (☎217-492-4150; www.nps.gov/liho; 426 S

7th St; ⏰8:30am-5pm) **FREE**, all in or near downtown. Oh, Springfield's Route 66 claim to fame? It's the birthplace of the corn dog (a cornmeal-battered, fried hot dog on a stick).

The Drive » Return to I-55, which supersedes Route 66 here, as in most of the state. The Route 66 Association of Illinois (www. il66assoc.org) tells you where to veer off for restored gas stations, vintage cafes and giant Lincoln statues. Near Edwardsville get on I-270, on which you'll swoop over the Mississippi River and enter Missouri.

---

❺ St Louis (p62)

Just over the border is St Louis, a can-do city that has launched westbound travelers for centuries. To ogle the city's most iconic attraction, exit I-270 onto Riverview Dr and point your car south toward the 630ft-tall **Gateway Arch** (☎314-655-1700; www. gatewayarch.com; tram ride adult/child $13/10; ⏰8am-10pm Jun-Aug, 9am-6pm

PHOTO UA / SHUTTERSTOCK ©

Sep-May, last tram 1hr before closing;), a graceful reminder of the city's role in westward expansion. For up-close views of the stainless-steel span and the Jefferson National Expansion Memorial surrounding it, turn left onto Washington Ave from Tucker Blvd (12th St). St Louis is also a great place to stretch those muscles, with a massive **park** to explore (☎314-367-7275; www. forestparkforever.org; bounded by Lindell Blvd, Kingshighway Blvd & I-64; ⏰6am-10pm).

The Drive » From St Louis, I-44 closely tracks – and often covers – chunks of original

---

> **DETOUR:**
> **OLD CHAIN OF ROCKS BRIDGE**
>
> **Start: ❹ Springfield**
>
> Before driving into Missouri, detour off I-270 at exit 3. Follow Hwy 3 (aka Lewis and Clark Blvd) south, turn right at the first stoplight and drive west to the 1929 **Old Chain of Rocks Bridge** (Old Chain of Rocks Rd; ⏰9am-sunset). Open only to pedestrians and cyclists these days, the mile-long span over the Mississippi River has a 22-degree angled bend (the cause of many a crash, hence the ban on cars). Hide your valuables and lock your car if you leave it to go exploring.

The Gateway Arch, St Louis

Mother Road. Take the interstate southwest to Stanton, then follow the signs to Meramec Caverns.

6 Meramec Caverns

Admit it: you're curious. Kitschy billboards have been touting **Meramec Caverns** (☏573-468-3166; www.americascave.com; I-44 exit 230, Stanton; adult/child $21/11; ⏰8:30am-7:30pm Jun-Aug, reduced hours Sep-May) for miles. The family-mobbed attraction and campground has lured road-trippers with its offbeat ads since 1933. From gold panning to riverboat rides, you'll find a day's worth of distractions, but don't miss the historically and geologically engaging cave tour. Note to kitsch seekers: the restaurant and gift store are actually inside the mouth of the cave.

The Drive ≫ Route 66 follows a series of winding county roads through wee towns such as Bourbon, Cuba and Devil's Elbow, all sticking close to I-44. After 100 miles or so, Lebanon makes a swell pit stop.

TRIP HIGHLIGHT

7 Lebanon

Most folks pull into town for the **Munger Moss Motel** (☏417-532-3111; www.mungermoss.com; 1336 E Rte 66; r from $60; ❄ 🛜 🏊). The 1940s lodging has a monster of a neon sign and atmospheric rooms, but more importantly it has Mother Road–loving owners who've been welcoming travelers for over 40 years. They can point you to the town's best root beer and antique shops, and the top spots to canoe amid the gorgeous Ozark hills.

The Drive ≫ Ditch I-44 west of Springfield, taking Hwy 96 to Civil War–era Carthage which has a historic town square

TOP TIP

Because Route 66 is no longer an official road, it doesn't appear on most maps. We've provided high-level directions, but you'll fare best using one of these additional resources: free turn-by-turn directions at www.historic66.com, or maps from the National Historic Route 66 Federation (www.national66.org).

and the 66 Drive-In Theater. From Joplin, follow Hwy 66 to Old Route 66 then hold tight: Kansas is on the horizon.

8 Kansas

The tornado-prone state holds a mere 13 miles of Mother Road (less than 1% of the total) but there's still a lot to see. First you'll pass through mine-scarred **Galena**, where a rusty old tow truck inspired animators from Pixar to create the character Mater in *Cars*. A few miles later, stop at the red-brick **Nelson's Old Riverton Store** (📞620-848-3330; www.eislerbros.com; 7109 SE Hwy 66, Riverton; 🕐7:30am-8pm Mon-Sat, noon-7pm Sun) and stock up on batteries, turkey sandwiches and Route 66 memorabilia. The 1925 property looks much like it did when first built – note the pressed-tin ceiling and the outhouse – and it's on the National Register of Historic Places. Cross Hwy 400 and continue to the **1923 Marsh Arch Bridge**, from where it's

3 miles south to **Baxter Springs**, site of a Civil War massacre and numerous bank robberies.

The Drive » Enter Oklahoma. From Afton, Route 66 parallels I-44 (now a tollway) through Vinita, home to a famed chicken-fried-steak cafe. Another 40 miles brings you to Claremore, home of cowboy Will Rogers, then to Catoosa, where the 80ft-long Blue Whale attracts camera-happy crowds. Tulsa rolls up soon after.

9 Tulsa (p67)

East 11th St takes you into and right through art-deco-rich Tulsa; be sure to look for the iconic neon wonder of the restored Meadow Gold sign at S Quaker Ave. To get a feel for what the city was like in its Route 66 days, head to the Brady Arts District, across the train tracks from downtown. Music clubs from the era still swing, and the offbeat **Woody Guthrie Center** (📞918-574-2710; www.woodyguthriecenter.org; 102 E MB Brady St; adult/child $8/6; 🕐10am-6pm Tue-Sun) and local jazz players impress.

The Drive » The rural route from Tulsa to Oklahoma City is one of the longest continuous stretches of Mother Road remaining (100 miles), a fine alternative to the I-44 tollway. As it approaches Oklahoma City, Route 66 follows Hwy 77 into town.

10 Oklahoma City (p68)

Bobby Troup called the city 'mighty pretty' in his classic tune 'Route 66,' but OKC is more cowboy than comely. Get in the spirit at the **National Cowboy & Western Heritage Museum** (📞405-478-2250; www.nationalcowboymuseum.org; 1700 NE 63rd St; adult/child $12.50/6; 🕐10am-5pm Mon-Sat, noon-5pm Sun). Other boots-and-chaps attractions are corralled south of downtown in Stockyards City, where you can watch a cattle auction, buy a custom-made cowboy hat or carve into savory sirloin. The *Field of Empty Chairs* at the **Oklahoma City National Memorial Museum** (www.oklahomacitynationalmemorial.org; 620 N Harvey Ave; adult/student $15/12; 🕐9am-6pm Mon-Sat, noon-6pm Sun, last ticket sold 1hr before close) is a moving reminder of those killed by a terrorist explosion here on April 19, 1995. On your way out of town, mosey into **Ann's Chicken Fry House** (📞405-943-8915; 4106 NW 39th St; mains $5-12; 🕐11am-

DIDIER FOTO / SHUTTERSTOCK ©

Oklahoma Route 66 Museum, Clinton

8:30pm Tue-Sat) for the time-honored specialty with cream gravy.

The Drive » From OKC, Route 66 follows Business I-40 for 20 miles to El Reno and its burgers. Sniff your way into town...

----

11 El Reno

The first fried-onion burger, a road-food classic, was served in 1926 in El Reno. Among several historic drive-ins and dives, try **Sid's Diner** (📞405-262-7757; 300 S Choctaw Ave, El Reno; mains from $4; 🕐7am-8pm Mon-Sat),

which has tables outside. Ground beef is combined with raw onions and then cooked and caramelized on the grill.

The Drive » The route hugs I-40, sometimes paralleling it to the north, through 60 miles of lonesome landscapes to Clinton.

TRIP HIGHLIGHT

12 Oklahoma Route 66 Museum

Flags from all eight Mother Road states fly high beside the memorabilia-filled **Oklahoma Route 66 Museum** (📞580-323-7866;

www.route66.org; 2229 W Gary Blvd, Clinton; adult/child $7/4; 🕐9am-7pm Mon-Sat, 1-6pm Sun May-Aug, reduced hours Sep-Apr) in Clinton. This fun-loving treasure trove, run by the Oklahoma Historical Society, isn't your typical mishmash of photos, clippings and knick-knacks (though there is an artifact-filled Cabinet of Curios). Instead, it uses music and videos to dramatize six decades of Route 66 history. Last exhibit? A faux-but-fun drive-in theater.

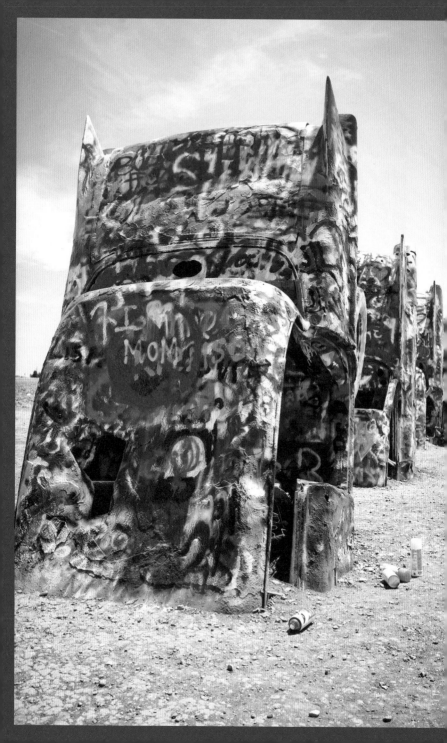

Central Route 66

2

Concrete wigwams, neon cowboys, lumbering dinosaurs: you'll get your kitsch on Route 66 following this storied stretch of the 'Mother Road' through Texas, New Mexico and Arizona.

TRIP HIGHLIGHTS

735 miles

Seligman
As quirky and loveable as it gets on Route 66

90 miles

Cadillac Ranch
Ten colorful Cadillacs take a nosedive into the dirt

Williams
10
8
6
3

START
McLean

Oatman
FINISH

615 miles

Meteor Crater
Peer over the edge of a mile-wide meteor crash site

560 miles

Petrified Forest National Park
Enjoy a sweeping park view at the Route 66 memorial

5–7 DAYS
900 MILES / 1448KM

GREAT FOR...

BEST TIME TO GO
April through September for the best conditions on the Colorado Plateau.

ESSENTIAL PHOTO
Capture the quirky concrete tipis at the Wigwam Motel in Holbrook, AZ.

BEST 2 DAYS
The natural wonders at Petrified Forest National Park and Meteor Crater.

Left Cadillac Ranch, created by Ant Farm (Lord, Michels and Marquez) © 1974 (p28)

Central Route 66

2

The Snow Cap Drive-In encapsulates everything that's cool about Route 66. There's personal interaction – did the guy behind the counter just squirt me with fake mustard? It's old-fashioned – why yes, I will get a malt. And it draws a diverse sampling of humanity – from a busload of bleary-eyed tourists to a horde of tough-looking biker dudes, all linked at the Snow Cap by the simple joy of an ice-cream cone.

❶ McLean

Beyond the towns, the great wide open of the Texas Panhandle is punctuated only by the occasional windmill, and the distinct odor of cattle feedlots. The Mother Road cuts across this emptiness for 178 miles, and the entire route has been superseded by I-40 – but there are a few noteworthy attractions.

The sprawling grasslands of Texas and other western cattle states were once open range, where steers and cow-

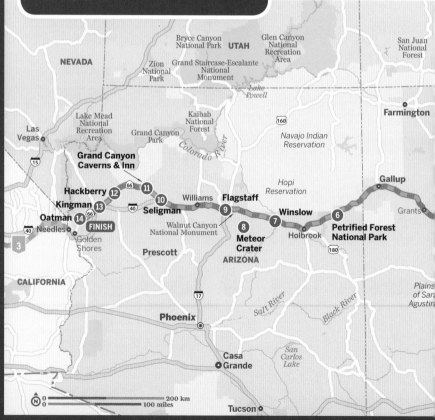

boys could wander where they darn well pleased. That all changed in the 1880s when the devil's rope – more commonly known as barbed wire – began dividing up the land into private parcels. The **Devil's Rope Museum** (www.barbwiremuseum. com; 100 Kingsley St, McLean; ⏰9am-4pm Mon-Sat Mar-Nov) in the battered town of McLean off exit 141 has vast barbed-wire displays and a quirky little room devoted to Route 66. The detailed map of the road in Texas is fascinating. Also worth a look are the

moving portraits of Dust Bowl damage and refugees from human-made environmental disaster.

The Drive ≫ I-40 west of McLean glides over low-rolling hills. The landscape flattens at Groom, home of the tilting water tower and a 19-story cross at Exit 112. Take Exit 96 for Conway to snap a photo of the forlorn VW Beetle Ranch, aka the Bug Ranch, on the south side of the interstate. It's 75 miles all told.

- - - - - - - - - - - - - - - - -

❷ Amarillo (p72)

This cowboy town holds a plethora of Route 66 sites: the **Big Texan Steak Ranch** (www.bigtexan.com; 7701 I-40 E,

exit 75; mains $10-40; ⏰7am-10:30pm; 🐾), the historic livestock auction and the **San Jacinto District**, which still has original Route 66 businesses.

As for the Big Texan, this hokey but classic attraction opened on Route 66 in 1960. It moved to its current location when I-40 opened in 1971 and has never looked back. The attention-grabbing gimmick here is the 'free 72oz steak' offer – you have to eat this enormous portion of cow plus a multitude of sides in under one hour, or you

ROUTE 66 **2 CENTRAL ROUTE 66**

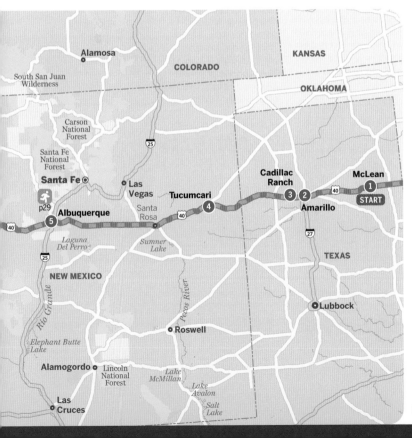

27

pay for the entire meal ($72). Contestants sit at a raised table to 'entertain' the other diners. Less than 10% pass the challenge. Insane eating aside, the ranch is a fine place to eat, and the steaks are excellent.

The Drive » Continue west on I-40. Take Exit 67, about 5 miles west of the edge of downtown Amarillo, then take S Western St under the interstate to Cadillac Ranch.

- - - - - - - - - - - - - - - - - -

TRIP HIGHLIGHT

③ Cadillac Ranch

Controversial local millionaire Stanley Marsh planted the shells of 10 Cadillacs in the deserted ground west of Amarillo in 1974 – an installation that's come to be known as **Cadillac Ranch**. He said he created it as a tribute to the golden age of car travel. The cars date from 1948 to 1959 – a period in which tail fins just kept getting

bigger and bigger. Come prepared: the accepted practice is to leave your own mark by spray painting on the cars. It can also get quite windy.

The Drive » Follow I-40 west 68 miles to the New Mexico border. Tucumcari – and its abundance of motel rooms – is 42 miles further.

- - - - - - - - - - - - - - - - - -

④ Tucumcari (p75)

A ranching and farming town sandwiched between the mesas and the plains, Tucumcari is home to one of the best-preserved sections of Route 66. It's a great place to drive through at night, when dozens of neon signs – relics of the town's Mother Road heyday – cast a crazy rainbow-colored glow. Tucumcari's Route 66 motoring legacy and other regional highlights are recorded on 35 murals in downtown and the surrounding area. Pick up a map for the murals at the

MARGARET W / SHUTTERSTOCK ©

Visitor Center (📞575-461-1694; www.tucumcarinm.com; 404 W Route 66; ⏱8:30am-5pm Mon-Fri).

The engaging **Mesalands Dinosaur Museum** (📞575-461-3466; www.mesalands.edu/community/dinosaur-museum; 222 E Laughlin St; adult/child $6.50/4; ⏱10am-6pm Tue-Sat Mar-Aug, noon-5pm Tue-Sat Sep-Feb; 👶) showcases real dinosaur bones and has hands-on exhibits for kids. Casts of dinosaur bones are done in bronze (not the usual plaster of paris), which shows fine detail.

The Drive » West on I-40, dry and windy plains spread into the distance, the horizon interrupted

GALLUP MURAL WALK

Take a walk around Gallup, an old Route 66 town on the I-40 between Albuquerque and the Arizona border, and experience its 136-year-old story through art. Starting from City Hall on the corner of W Aztec Ave and S 2nd St you'll see plenty of buildings sporting giant murals, both abstract and realist, that memorialize special events in Gallup's roller-coaster history. The city's mural painting tradition started in the 1930s as part of President Franklin D Roosevelt's Great Depression Work Projects Administration (WPA) program. It continues to this day, with 21st-century artists reimagining the story of Gallup through contemporary eyes.

Blue Mesa Trail, Petrified Forest National Park (p30)

by flat-topped mesas. To stretch your legs, take Exit 277 from I-40 to Route 66, downtown Santa Rosa and the Route 66 Auto Museum, which has upward of 35 cars from the 1920s through the 1960s, all in beautiful condition. It's 174 miles.

-----

⑤ Albuquerque (p75)

After 1936, Route 66 was re-aligned from its original path, which linked north through Santa Fe, to a direct line west into Albuquerque. Today, the city's **Central Ave** follows the post-1937 route. It passes through **Nob Hill**, the university, downtown and **Old Town**.

The patioed **Kelly's Brewery** (www.kellys brewpub.com; 3222 Central Ave SE; ⏲8am-10:30pm

Sun-Thu, to midnight Fri & Sat), in now-trendy Nob Hill, was an Art Moderne gas station on the Route,

 DETOUR: SANTA FE

Start: ⑤ **Albuquerque**

New Mexico's capital city (p75) is an oasis of art and culture lifted 7000ft above sea level, against the backdrop of the Sangre de Christo Mountains. It was on Route 66 until 1937, when a realignment left it by the wayside. It's well worth the detour to see the **Georgia O'Keeffe Museum** (☎505-946-1000; www. okeeffemuseum.org; 217 Johnson St; adult/child $12/free; ⏲10am-5pm Sat-Thu, to 7pm Fri), to fork into uberhot green chile dishes in the superb restaurants, and to stroll past the town's churches and galleries. Route 66 follows the Old Pecos Trail (NM466) into town.

commissioned in 1939. West of **I-25**, look for the spectacular tile-and-wood artistry of the **KiMo Theatre** (Map p76; 505-768-3544; www.cabq.gov/kimo; 423 Central Ave NW), across from the old **Indian Trading Post**. This 1927 icon of pueblo-deco architecture blends American Indian and art deco design. It also screens classic movies like *Singin' in the Rain* and *2001: A Space Odyssey*. For prehistoric designs, take **Exit 154**, just west of downtown, and drive north 3 miles to **Petroglyph National Monument** (www.nps.gov/petr; 6001 Unser Blvd NW; visitor center 8am-5pm), which has more than 23,000 ancient rock etchings.

The Drive » Route 66 dips from I-40 into Gallup, becoming the main drag, lined with beautifully renovated buildings, including the 1928 Spanish Colonial El Morro Theatre. From Gallup, it's 21 miles to Arizona. Once in Arizona, take Exit 311 for Petrified Forest National Park. It's 211 miles all up.

TRIP HIGHLIGHT

6 Petrified Forest National Park

The 'trees' of the **Petrified Forest** (928-524-6228; www.nps.gov/pefo; vehicle $20, walk-in/bicycle/motorcycle $10; 7am-7pm Mar-Sep, shorter hours Oct-Feb) are fragmented, fossilized 225-million-year-old logs scattered over a vast area of arid grassland. Many are huge – up to 6ft in di-

ameter – and at least one spans a ravine to form a natural bridge. The trees arrived via major floods, only to be buried beneath silica-rich volcanic ash before they could decompose. Groundwater dissolved the silica, carried it through the logs and crystallized into solid, sparkly quartz mashed up with iron, carbon, manganese and other minerals. Uplift and erosion eventually exposed the logs.

The park, which straddles the I-40, has an entrance at Exit 311 in the north and another off Hwy 180 in the south. A 28-mile paved scenic road, Park Rd, links the two. To avoid backtracking, westbound travelers should start in the north, eastbound travelers in the south.

The Drive » Drive west 26 miles to Holbrook, a former Wild West town now home to rock shops and the photo-ready Wigwam Motel, which was added to the National Register of Historic Places in 2002. If someone is on the grounds before the 4pm check-in, they'll probably let you peek inside one of the wigwams. Continue west on I-40; it's another 33 miles.

------

7 Winslow

Thanks to The Eagles' 1972 hit 'Take It Easy' (their first single release), lonesome little Winslow is now a popular stop on the tourist track. Pose with the life-sized bronze statue of a hitchhiker backed by a charmingly

---

SCENIC DRIVE: PETRIFIED FOREST NATIONAL PARK

The leisurely Park Rd, which travels through the park, has about 15 pullouts with interpretive signs and some short trails. North of I-40, enjoy sweeping views of the Painted Desert, where nature presents a hauntingly beautiful palette, especially at sunset. After Park Rd turns south, keep a lookout for the roadside display about Route 66, just north of the interstate.

The 3-mile loop drive out to Blue Mesa has 360-degree views of spectacular badlands, log falls and logs with the leathery texture of elephant skin balancing atop hills.

Two trails near the southern entrance provide the best access for close-ups of the petrified logs: the 0.6-mile Long Logs Trail, which has the larger concentration, and the 0.4-mile Giant Logs Trail, which is entered through the **Rainbow Forest Museum** (928-524-6822; www.nps.gov; 6618 Petrified Forest Rd; 7am-7pm Mar-Sep, shorter hours Oct-Feb) and sports the park's largest log.

hokey *trompe l'oeil* mural of that famous girl in a flatbed Ford at the corner of **2nd St** and **Kinsley Ave**.

The Drive » Twenty miles west of Winslow, take Exit 233 off I-40 and drive 6 miles south through cattle country, following the signs for Meteor Crater.

----

⑧ Meteor Crater

Some 50,000 years ago an asteroid travelling at 26,000mph crashed here, blasting a hole more than 550ft deep and nearly 1 mile across. Today the privately owned **crater** (☎800-289-5898, 928-289-5898; www.meteorcrater. com; Meteor Crater Rd; adult/senior/child 6-17yr $18/16/9; ◷7am-7pm Jun–mid-Sep, 8am-5pm mid-Sep–May; P ♿) is a major tourist attraction with exhibits about meteorites, crater geology and the Apollo astronauts who used its lunar-like surface to train for their moon missions. You're not allowed to go down into the crater, but there are a few lookout points as well as guided one-hour rim-walking tours (free with admission). Look for the glinting piece of a plane that crashed inside the crater.

The Drive » Follow I-40 to Exit 204 and pick up Route 66 into Flagstaff. This is also the exit for Walnut Canyon National Monument. From the east, Route 66 passes a lengthy swath of cheap indie motels as well as the Museum Club (3404 E Rte 66), a log-cabin-style roadhouse that's been refreshing road-trippers since 1936.

ROAD TRIP READS

John Steinbeck's 1939 novel *Grapes of Wrath* is the definitive tale of travel on the Mother Road during the Dust Bowl era. Woody Guthrie's *Bound for Glory*, first published in 1943, is the road-trip autobiography of the revered folk singer during the Depression. Several museums and bookshops along Route 66 stock American Indian, Old West and pioneer writing with ties to the old highway.

----

⑨ Flagstaff (p87)

This cultured college town still has an Old West heart. At the **Visitor Center** (☎800-842-7293, 928-213-2951; www.flagstaffarizona.org; 1 E Rte 66; ◷8am-5pm Mon-Sat, 9am-4pm Sun), inside the historic train station, pick up the free Route 66 walking-tour guide. One building of note on the tour is the **Downtowner Motel**, formerly a brothel and now the Grand Canyon International Youth Hostel. Just north of Route 66 are two century-old hotels: the **Hotel Monte Vista** (☎928-779-6971; www.hotelmontevista.com; 100 N San Francisco St; r/ste from $115/145; ❄ 🛜) and the **Weatherford Hotel** (Map p87; ☎928-779-1919; www.weatherfordhotel.com; 23 N Leroux St; s/d from $115/155; ❄ 🛜). Both have plenty of character, not to mention convivial watering holes and lively ghosts.

If you're interested in architecture, stop by **Riordan Mansion State Historic Park** (☎928-779-4395; https://azstateparks. com/riordan-mansion; 409 W Riordan Rd; tour adult/child 7-13yr $10/5; ◷9:30am-5pm May-Oct, 10:30am-5pm Thu-Mon Nov-Apr), practically part of the **Northern Arizona University** campus. Having made a fortune from their Arizona Lumber Company, brothers Michael and Timothy Riordan built this striking log-slab mansion in 1904. Its Craftsman-style design is the work of architect Charles Whittlesey, who also designed **El Tovar** (www.nps.gov/grca; Village Loop Dr; 🚌Village) on the Grand Canyon's South Rim.

The Drive » Continue west on I-40 and Route 66 to Williams, home of the Grand Canyon Railway and the last community along Route 66 to be bypassed by I-40. Route 66 runs one way through town, from west to east – you'll need to take parallel Railroad Ave. rejoin I-40, then leave it again at Exit 139. All up, it's a 76-mile drive.

----

⑩ Seligman

This town takes its Route 66 heritage seriously – or with a squirt of fake mustard, thanks to the Delgadillo brothers, who for decades were the Mother Road's biggest boosters. Juan sadly passed away in 2004, but evergreen Angel and his wife still run **Angel & Vilma's Original Route 66 Gift Shop** (☎928-422-3352; www.route66giftshop.com; 22265 E Rte 66; ◷9am-5pm winter, 8am-6pm rest of the year), where you can poke around for souvenirs and admire license plates sent in by fans from all over the world. The much-lamented Juan used to rule prankishly supreme over **Delgadillo's Snow Cap Drive-In** (☎928-422-3291; 301 Rte 66; mains $5-6.50; ◷10am-6pm Mar-Nov), a Route 66 institution serving burgers, ice cream and pranks that's now run by his children Cecilia and John.

The Drive » The Mother Road rolls northwest through dry, scrub-covered country, passing

Burma Shave signs and lonely trains. After a drive of 25 miles, look for the kitsch dinosaur at mile marker 115.

⓫ Grand Canyon Caverns & Inn

An elevator drops 210ft underground to artificially lit limestone caverns and the skeletal remains of a prehistoric ground sloth at **Grand Canyon Caverns** (☎855-498-6969, 928-422-3223; www.grandcanyoncaverns.com; Mile 115, Rte 66; tour adult/child from $16/11; ◷8am-6pm May-Sep, call for off-season hours). While there's no connection with the Grand Canyon beyond the name, this can be a cool and diverting escape from the summer heat, and is always popular with kids. And if you really want to make an night of it, $850 buys repose

in the Cavern Suite. This underground 'room' has two double beds, a sitting area and multicolored lamps. If you ever wanted to cast yourself in one of those postapocalyptic survival movies, here's your chance!

The Drive » Continue west through Peach Springs, Truxton and Valentine for 35 miles.

⓬ Hackberry

Tiny, sleepy Hackberry is one of the few still-kicking settlements on this segment of the Mother Road's original alignment. Inside an eccentrically remodeled gas station dating from 1934 is the **Hackberry General Store** (☎928-769-2605; www.hackberrygeneralstore.com; 11255 E Route 66, Hackberry; ◷9am-6pm Apr-Oct, 10am-5pm Nov-Mar; P). Originated by highway memorialist Robert Waldmire, the store is a great place to stop for a cold drink and Route 66 memorabilia. Check out the vintage petrol pumps, cars faded by decades of hot desert light, old toilet seats and rusted-out ironwork.

The Drive » From here, Route 66 arcs southwest, back toward I-40, then barrels into Kingman, which is 27 miles away.

⓭ Kingman

Founded in the heady 1880s railway days, Kingman is a quiet place today, but popular with Route 66

Flagstaff's historic station (p31)
NICK FOX / SHUTTERSTOCK ©

buffs for its well-preserved motels and other heyday architecture. A 1907 powerhouse holds the **Visitor Center** (📞866-427-7866, 928-753-6106; www.gokingman.com; 120 W Andy Devine Ave; ⊙8am-5pm) and the small but engaging **Route 66 Museum** (📞928-753-9889; www.gokingman.com; 120 W Andy Devine Ave; adult/senior/child 12yr & under $4/3/free; ⊙9am-5pm, last entry at 4pm), which really brings the glory days of the Mother Road to life. You could also check out the **former Methodist church** at 5th and Spring St, where Clark Gable and Carole Lombard eloped in 1939.

In Kingman Route 66 is also called Andy Devine Ave, named after the hometown hero who acted in Hollywood classics like *Stagecoach*, in which he played the perpetually befuddled stagecoach driver.

The Drive » Route 66/Hwy 10 corkscrews 29 miles up through the rugged Black Mountains, passing falling rocks, cacti and tumbleweeds on its way over Sitgreaves Pass (3523ft) to the old mining town of Oatman.

----

⑭ Oatman

Since the veins of ore ran dry in 1942, crusty Oatman has reinvented

HISTORY OF THE MOTHER ROAD

Launched in 1926, Route 66 stretched from Chicago to Los Angeles, linking a ribbon of small towns and country byways as it rolled across eight states. The road gained notoriety during the Great Depression, when migrant farmers followed it west from the Dust Bowl across the Great Plains. The nickname 'The Mother Road' first appeared in John Steinbeck's 1939 novel about the era, *The Grapes of Wrath*. Meanwhile, unemployed young men were hired to pave the final stretches of muddy road. They completed the job, as it turns out, just in time for WWII and the flood of soldiers and factory workers that took the road to fortune and despair. Things got a little more fun in the 1950s, when newfound prosperity prompted Americans to hit the open road. Sadly, just as things got going, the Feds rolled out the interstate system, which eventually caused the Mother Road's demise. The very last town to be bypassed by an interstate was Arizona's Williams, in 1984.

itself as a movie set and Wild West tourist trap, complete with staged gun fights (daily at 1:30pm, and sometimes 3:30pm) and gift stores with names like **Fast Fanny's Place** and the **Classy Ass**.

Speaking of asses, there are plenty of them (the four-legged kind, that is) roaming the streets. Placid and endearing, they're the descendants of pack animals left by the early miners. These burros may beg for food, but do not feed them your lunch leftovers; instead, buy healthier hay

cubes from nearby stores. Squeezed among the shops is the 1902 **Oatman Hotel** (📞928-768-4408; 181 Main St; ⊙10am-6pm Mon-Fri, 8am-6pm Sat & Sun), a surprisingly modest shack (no longer renting rooms) where Clark Gable and Carole Lombard spent their wedding night in 1939. On July 4 the town holds a sidewalk egg-frying contest. It gets quite warm here in summer.

From here, Route 66 twists down to Golden Shores and the I-40.

Western Route 66

3

From historic Needles in the east to the sparkling waters of the mighty Pacific, search for your own American dream along California's stretch of the Mother Road.

TRIP HIGHLIGHTS

300 miles

Hollywood
Get your kicks in
Tinseltown

80 miles

Amboy
The big sky and empty
byways are starkly
photogenic

START
Needles

3

● Victorville

● San
Bernardino

10
● **Los Angeles**
11
FINISH

Santa Monica
End this epic trip on
the Pacific shore

310 miles

3–4 DAYS
350 MILES / 565KM

GREAT FOR...

BEST TIME TO GO

Spring, for cruising
with the windows
down before the heat
of summer.

**ESSENTIAL
PHOTO**

Laying down on the
faded blacktop next to
a Route 66 sign.

BEST ROAD
National Trails
Hwy between Goffs
and Amboy is the
quintessential middle-
of-nowhere stretch.

Western Route 66

3

For generations of Americans, California, with its sparkling waters and sunny skies, was the promised land for road-trippers on Route 66. Follow their tracks through the gauntlet of Mojave Desert ghost towns, railway whistle-stops like Barstow and Victorville, and across the Cajon Summit. Finally, wind through the LA Basin and put it in park near the crashing ocean waves at the end of Santa Monica Pier.

❶ Needles

At the Arizona border south of I-40 the arched **Old Trails Bridge** (🕓 no public access) welcomes the Mother Road to California under endless blue skies. You might recognize the bridge: the Depression-era Joad family used it to cross the Colorado River in the movie version of John Steinbeck's novel *Grapes of Wrath*. Drive west past Needles, a dusty throw-back railroad town with a historic depot down by the river. Frozen in a

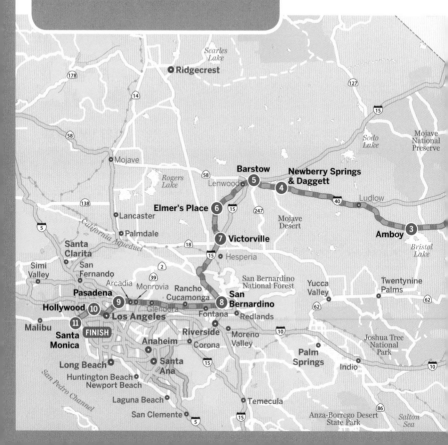

half-restored state, the **El Garces Depot** is one of only a few frontier-era Harvey Houses left standing in the American West. The Harvey Houses were a chain of railway hotels and restaurants popular in the late 19th and early 20th centuries that were famed for traveling waitresses, as portrayed by Judy Garland in the 1946 MGM musical *The Harvey Girls*. Head a bit south on Broadway and you'll pass a freshly restored **66 Motel Sign** at the corner of Desnok Street – a great photo.

The Drive 》 About 15 miles west of Needles, follow Hwy 95 north of I-40 for 6 miles, then turn left onto Goffs Rd. You'll inevitably be running alongside a long locomotive – this is a primary rail shipping route to the West Coast.

----

2 Goffs

The shade of cotton-wood trees make the 1914 Mission-style **Goffs Schoolhouse** (☏760-733-4482; www.mdhca.org; 37198 Lanfair Rd, Essex; ☺9am-4pm Sat-Mon Oct-Jun, call to confirm; **P**) a soothing stop along this sun-drenched stretch of highway. It stands as part of the best-preserved pioneer settlement in the Mojave Desert (although to be quite honest it looks a bit like an empty Taco Bell). Browsing the black-and-white photographs of hardscrabble Dust Bowl migrants gives an evocative glimpse into tough life on the edge of the Mojave.

The Drive 》 If the bridge beyond Goffs has been restored, keep going on Goffs Rd through Fenner, crossing under I-40; otherwise, backtrack to I-40 via Hwy 95. Turn right onto National Old Trails Hwy (known as National Trails Hwy on some maps and signs) and drive for about an hour, passing abandoned graffiti-covered service stations and vintage signs rusting in the sun.

TRIP HIGHLIGHT

3 Amboy

Potholed and crumbling in a romantic way, the USA's original trans-national highway was established in 1912, more than a decade before Route 66 first ran through here. The rutted highway races through tiny towns, sparsely scattered across the Mojave. Only a few landmarks interrupt the horizon, including **Roy's Motel & Cafe** (www.rt66roys. com; National Old Trails Hwy, Amboy; ☺7am-8pm, seasonal variations; **P**), a landmark watering hole for decades of Route 66 travelers. If you'll believe the lore, Roy once cooked his famous Route 66 double cheeseburger on the hood of a '63 Mercury. Although the motel is abandoned, the gas station and cafe are occasionally open. It's east of **Amboy Crater** (☏760-326-7000; www.blm. gov/ca; ☺sunrise-sunset; **P**), an almost perfectly symmetrical volcanic cinder cone. You can hike to the top, but not in summer and it's best to avoid the midday sun – the 3-mile round-trip hike doesn't have a stitch of shade.

The Drive 》 From Amboy travel almost 30 miles along National Old Trails Highway to Ludlow. Turn right onto Crucero Rd and pass under I-40, then take the north frontage road west and turn left at Lavic Rd. Back on the south side of I-40, keep heading west on National Old Trails Hwy. The entire trip takes about one hour and 45 minutes.

TOP TIP:
NAVIGATING THE
MOTHER ROAD

Nostalgia for the Mother Road draws its shares of completists who want to drive every inch. For Route 66 enthusiasts who need to cover every mile, a free turn-by-turn driving guide is available online at www.historic66.com. Also surf to http://route66ca.org for more historical background, photos and info about special events.

④ Newberry Springs & Daggett

The highway passes under I-40 on its way through **Daggett**, site of the harsh California inspection station faced by Dust Bowl refugees in *Grapes of Wrath*. Today there ain't much action, but it's a windswept, picturesque place. Pay your respects to early desert adventurers at the old **Stone Hotel** (35630 Santa Fe St, Daggett; ⊙ no public entry; P). This late-19th-century hotel once housed miners, desert explorers and wanderers, including Sierra Nevada naturalist John Muir and con artist 'Death Valley Scotty'. Then make your way out of town to visit **Calico Ghost Town** (☏800-862-2542; www.calicotown.com; 36600 Ghost Town Rd, Yermo; adult/child $8/5; ⊙9am-5pm; P ♿). This endearingly hokey Old West attraction sets a cluster of reconstructed pioneer-era buildings amid ruins of a late-19th-century silver mining town. You'll pay extra to go gold panning, take a mine tour or ride a narrow-gauge railway. Old-timey heritage celebrations include Civil War reenactments and a bluegrass 'hootenanny.'

The Drive ≫ From Daggett, drive west to Nebo Rd, turning left to rejoin I-40. You'll drive about 4 miles before taking the exit for E Main St.

⑤ Barstow

Exit the interstate onto Main St, which runs through Barstow, a railroad settlement and historic crossroads, where murals adorn empty buildings downtown. Follow 1st St north across the Mojave River over a trestle bridge to the 1911 Harvey House, nicknamed **Casa del Desierto**, designed by Western architect Mary Colter. Inside is the **Route 66 'Mother Road' Museum** (☏760-255-1890; www.route66museum.org; 681 N 1st St; ⊙10am-4pm Fri & Sat, 11am-4pm Sun, or by appointment; P ♿), displaying black-and-white historical photographs and odds and ends of everyday life in the early 20th century. Next door is the small **Western America Railroad Museum** (WARM; ☏760-256-9276; www.barstowrailmuseum.org; 685 N 1st St; ⊙11am-4pm Fri-Sun; P).

The Drive ≫ Leaving Barstow via Main St, rejoin the National Old Trails Hwy west. It curves alongside the Mojave River through Lenwood. After about 25 miles you'll arrive at Elmer's Place.

⑥ Elmer's Place

Loved by Harley bikers, this rural byway is like a scavenger hunt for Mother Road ruins, including antique filling stations and tumbledown motor courts. Colorful as a box of crayons, **Elmer's Place** (24266 National Trails Hwy, Oro Grande; ⊙outside 24hr; P) is a roadside folk-art collection of 'bottle trees,' made from recycled soda pop and beer containers, telephone poles and railroad signs. Elmer Long, who was a career man at the cement factory you'll pass just out of town, is the proprietor and cracked artistic genius. If you see someone with a long white beard and leathery skin cementing a statue of a bronze deity to some elk antlers, you've found the right guy. Want to leave a little part of yourself along Route 66? Bring a little something for Elmer Long's colorful forest, constructed lovingly out of little pieces of junk.

The Drive » Cross over the Mojave River on a 1930s steel-truss bridge, then roll into downtown Victórville, a trip of almost 12 miles.

7 Victorville

Opposite the railroad tracks in quiet little Victorville, visitors poke around a mishmash of historical exhibits and contemporary art inside the **California Route 66 Museum** (📞760-951-0436; www.califrt66museum.org; 16825 South D St, Victorville; donations welcome; ⏰10am-4pm Thu-Sat & Mon,

11am-3pm Sun; P 🚻). The museum building itself was once the Red Rooster Cafe, a famous Route 66 roadhouse. It's a bit of a cluttered nostalgia trip – piled with old signs and roadside memorabilia – but worth a quick look.

The Drive » Get back on I-15 south over the daunting Cajon Summit. If you're hungry, pull off in Hesperia at the Summit Inn, a classic diner. Descending into San Bernardino, take I-215 and exit at Devore. Follow Cajon Blvd to Mt Vernon Ave, detour east on Base Line St and go left onto 'E' St. This trip takes about 40 minutes.

8 San Bernadino

Look for the Golden Arches outside the unofficial **First McDonald's Museum** (📞909-885-6324; www.facebook.com/firstoriginal mcdonaldsmuseum; 1398 N E St, San Bernardino; by donation; ⏰10am-5pm; P 🚻). It was here that salesman Ray Kroc dropped in to sell Richard and Maurice McDonald a mixer. Eventually Kroc bought the rights to the brothers' name and built an empire. Half of the museum is devoted to Route 66, with particularly

Calico Ghost Town (p38), outside of Daggett

City Hall, Pasadena

interesting photographs and maps. Turn west on 5th St, leaving San Bernardino via Foothill Blvd, which continues straight into the urban sprawl of greater Los Angeles. It's a long haul west to Pasadena, with stop-and-go traffic most of the way, but there are more than a handful of gems to uncover. Cruising through Fontana, birthplace of the Hells Angels biker club, pause for a photo by the **Giant Orange** (15395 Foothill Blvd, Fontana; ⊘ closed to public; **P**), a 1930s juice stand of the kind that was once a fixture alongside SoCal's citrus groves.

The Drive ›› Stay on Route 66 as it detours briefly from Foothill Blvd onto Alosta Ave in Glendora, where you can stop for lunch at the Hat. Shortly after 66 rejoins Foothill Blvd in Azusa, continue onto Huntington Dr in Duarte, where a boisterous Route 66 parade happens in September.

- - - - - - - - - - - - - - - -

⑨ Pasadena

Just before you reach Pasadena, you'll pass through **Arcadia**, home to the 1930s **Santa Anita Park** (⌨ tickets 626-574-6366, tour info 626-574-6677; www.santaanita.com; 285 W Huntington Dr; adult/child from $5/free; ⊘ racing season Christmas–mid-Apr, late Sep–early Nov, tram tours

8:30am & 9:45am Sat & Sun during racing season; 🛜 🚻). This track is where the Marx Brothers' *A Day at the Races* was filmed (and more recently the HBO series *Luck*) and where legendary thoroughbred Seabiscuit once ran. Stepping through the soaring art-deco entrance into the grandstands, you'll feel like a million bucks – even if you don't win any wagers. During race season, free tram tours go behind the scenes into the jockeys' room and training areas; reservations required. Continue along Colorado Blvd into wealthy **Old Pasadena**, a bustling shopping district west of Arroyo Pkwy, where boutiques and cafes are housed in handsomely restored historic Spanish Colonial Revival–style buildings.

The Drive » Join the jet-set modern world on the Pasadena Fwy (Hwy 110), which streams south into LA. One of the first freeways in the US, it's a truck-free state historic freeway – the whole trip will take less than 20 minutes. Take the Santa Monica Blvd exit, then follow Sunset Blvd northwest to Santa Monica Blvd westbound.

TRIP HIGHLIGHT

⑩ Hollywood (p96)

Like a resurrected diva of the silver screen, Hollywood is making a comeback. Although it hasn't recaptured the Golden Age glamour that brought would-be starlets cruising here on Route 66, this historic neighborhood is still worth visiting for its restored movie palaces, unique museums and the pink stars on the **Hollywood Walk of Fame** (Map p98; www.walkoffame.com; Hollywood Blvd; [M]Red Line to Hollywood/Highland). The exact track that Route 66 ran through the neighborhood isn't possible to follow these days (it changed officially a couple times and has long been paved over). Start exploring at the

Hollywood & Highland

(www.hollywoodandhighland.com; 6801 Hollywood Blvd; ⊙10am-10pm Mon-Sat, to 7pm Sun; [🚻]; [M]Red Line to Hollywood/Highland) shopping, dining and entertainment complex, north of Santa Monica Blvd, in the center of the action. The **Los Angeles Visitor Information Center** (Map p98; ☏323-467-6412; www.discoverlosangeles.com; Hollywood & Highland, 6801 Hollywood Blvd; ⊙8am-10pm Mon-Sat, 9am-7pm Sun; [M]Red Line to Hollywood/Highland) is upstairs. Travelers looking for a fun, creepy communion with stars of yesteryear should stroll the **Hollywood Forever Cemetery** (☏323-469-1181; www.hollywoodforever.com; 6000 Santa Monica Blvd; ⊙usually 8:30am-5pm, flower shop 9am-5pm Mon-Fri, to 4pm Sat & Sun; [P]) next to Paramount Pictures, which is crowded with famous 'immortals,' including Rudolph Valentino, Tyrone Power, Jayne Mansfield and Cecil B DeMille. Buy a map at the flower shop near the entrance.

The Drive » Follow Santa Monica Blvd west for 13 miles to reach the end of the road – it meets Ocean Ave at Palisades Park. Hwy 1 is downhill from Ocean Ave heading north. The pier is a few blocks to the south.

TRIP HIGHLIGHT

⑪ Santa Monica (p114)

This is the end of the line: Route 66 reaches its finish, over 2200 miles from its starting point in Chicago, on an ocean bluff in **Palisades Park** (☏800-544-5319; Ocean Ave btwn Colorado Ave & San Vicente Blvd; ⊙5am-midnight), where a Will Rogers Hwy memorial plaque marks the official end of the Mother Road. Celebrate on **Santa Monica Pier** (☏310-458-8901; www.santamonicapier.org; [🚻]), where you can ride a 1920s carousel featured in *The Sting,* gently touch tidepool critters at the **Santa Monica Pier Aquarium** (☏310-393-6149; www.healthebay.org; 1600 Ocean Front Walk; adult/child $5/free; ⊙2-6pm Tue-Fri, 12:30-6pm Sat & Sun; [🚻]; [M]Expo Line to Downtown Santa Monica) and soak up a sunset atop the solar-powered Ferris wheel at **Pacific Park** (☏310-260-8744; www.pacpark.com; 380 Santa Monica Pier; per ride $5-10, all-day pass adult/child under 8yr $32/18; ⊙daily, seasonal hours vary; [🚻]; [M]Expo Line to Downtown Santa Monica). Year-round carnival rides include the West Coast's only oceanfront steel roller coaster – a thrilling ride to end this classic trip.

Destinations

Illinois (p44)
Start your nostalgic, kitschy adventure in downtown Chicago, before making your way to historic Springfield, once home to 'Honest Abe' Lincoln.

Missouri to Oklahoma (p62)
On your way along the Mother Road, take in some quintessential American cities: St Louis, the 'gateway to the West'; oil capital Tulsa; and cowboy hotspot Oklahoma City.

Texas to Arizona (p72)
From the Grand Canyon to Wheeler Peak, awe-inspiring natural sites abound in the Southwest, but its cities offer surprising delights: from steak-lovin' Amarillo to creative Santa Fe to hiking haven Flagstaff, there's much to experience.

California (p96)
After zooming past ghost towns in the Mojave Desert, fulfill your Hollywood dreams and take in the City of Angels, before ending your journey on the sunny beaches of Santa Monica.

Chicago (p44)
RUDY BALASKO / SHUTTERSTOCK ©

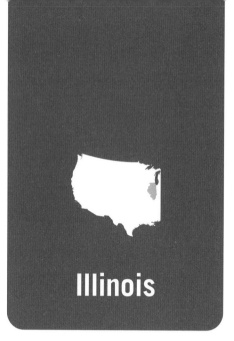

Illinois

Chicago dominates the state with its sky-high architecture and superlative museums, restaurants and music clubs. But venturing further afield leads down a trail of corn dogs, pies and drive-in movie theaters down Route 66.

ℹ️ Information

Illinois Highway Conditions (www.getting aroundillinois.com)

Illinois Office of Tourism (www.enjoyillinois. com)

Illinois State Park Information (www.dnr. illinois.gov) State parks are free to visit. Camp-sites cost $6 to $35; some accept reservations (www.reserveamerica.com; fee $5).

Chicago

Steely skyscrapers, rocking festivals, top chefs – the Windy City will blow you away with its low-key cultured awesomeness.

⦿ Sights

⦿ The Loop

Art Institute of Chicago   MUSEUM
(🕿 312-443-3600; www.artic.edu; 111 S Michigan Ave; adult/child $25/free; ⊙ 10:30am-5pm Fri-Wed, to 8pm Thu; 🚹; Ⓜ Brown, Orange, Green, Purple, Pink Line to Adams) The Art Institute's collec-tion of impressionist and post-impressionist paintings rivals those in France, and the number of surrealist works is tremendous.

Download the free app for DIY audio tours; it offers several quick-hit jaunts, from high-lights (including Georges Seurat's *A Sunday Afternoon on the Island of La Grande Jatte* and Edward Hopper's *Nighthawks*) to archi-tecture and pop art tours. Allow two hours to browse the museum's must-sees; art buffs should allocate much longer.

Millennium Park   PARK
(🕿 312-742-1168; www.millenniumpark.org; 201 E Randolph St; ⊙ 6am-11pm; 🚹; Ⓜ Brown, Orange, Green, Purple, Pink Line to Washington/Wabash) The city's showpiece is a trove of free and arty sights. It includes **Pritzker Pavilion**, Frank Gehry's swooping silver band shell, which hosts free concerts most nights in summer (6:30pm; bring a picnic and bot-tle of wine); Anish Kapoor's beloved silvery sculpture **Cloud Gate**, aka the 'Bean'; and Jaume Plensa's **Crown Fountain**, a de facto water park that projects video images of lo-cals spitting water, gargoyle style.

Willis Tower   TOWER
(🕿 312-875-9696; www.theskydeck.com; 233 S Wacker Dr; adult/child $23/15; ⊙ 9am-10pm Mar-Sep, 10am-8pm Oct-Feb; Ⓜ Brown, Orange, Purple, Pink Line to Quincy) It's Chicago's tallest build-

ing, and the 103rd-floor Skydeck puts you high into the heavens. Take the ear-popping, 70-second elevator ride to the top and then step onto one of the glass-floored ledges jutting out in mid-air for a knee-buckling perspective straight down. On clear days the view sweeps over four states. The entrance is on Jackson Blvd. Queues can take up to an hour on busy days (peak times are in summer, between 11am and 4pm Friday through Sunday).

⊙ Near North & Navy Pier

Navy Pier   WATERFRONT

(☑312-595-7437; www.navypier.com; 600 E Grand Ave; ☺10am-10pm Sun-Thu, to midnight Fri & Sat Jun-Aug, 10am-8pm Sun-Thu, to 10pm Fri & Sat Sep-May; ♿; Ⓜ Red Line to Grand) **FREE** Half-mile-long Navy Pier is one of Chicago's most-visited attractions, sporting a 196ft **Ferris wheel** (adult/child $15/12) and other carnival rides ($6 to $15 each), an **IMAX theater** (☑312-595-5629; www.imax.com; 600 E Grand Ave; tickets $15-22), a beer garden and lots of chain restaurants. Locals groan over its commercialization, but its lakefront view and cool breezes can't be beat. The fireworks displays on summer Wednesdays (9:30pm) and Saturdays (10:15pm) are a treat too.

Chicago Children's Museum   MUSEUM

(☑312-527-1000; www.chicagochildrensmuseum. org; 700 E Grand Ave; admission $14; ☺10am-5pm, to 8pm Thu; ♿; Ⓜ Red Line to Grand) Designed to challenge the imaginations of toddlers to 10-year-olds, this colorful museum near Navy Pier's main entrance gives young visitors enough hands-on exhibits to keep them climbing and creating for hours. Among the favorites, Dinosaur Expedition explores the world of paleontology and lets kids excavate 'bones.' They can also climb a ropey schooner; bowl in a faux alley; get wet in the waterways (and learn about hydroelectric power); and use real tools to build things in the Tinkering Lab.

⊙ Gold Coast

360° Chicago   OBSERVATORY

(☑888-875-8439; www.360chicago.com; 875 N Michigan Ave, John Hancock Center, 94th fl; adult/child $20.50/13.50; ☺9am-11pm; Ⓜ Red Line to Chicago) In many ways the view here surpasses the one at Willis Tower (p44). The 94th-floor lookout has informative displays and the TILT feature (floor-to-ceiling windows that you stand in as they tip out over the ground; it costs $7 extra and is less exciting than it sounds). Not interested in such frivolities? Shoot straight up to the 96th-floor Signature Lounge (p56), where the view comes free with the purchase of a drink ($8 to $16).

Museum of Contemporary Art   MUSEUM

(MCA; ☑312-280-2660; www.mcachicago.org; 220 E Chicago Ave; adult/child $15/free; ☺10am-8pm Tue, to 5pm Wed-Sun; Ⓜ Red Line to Chicago)

ILLINOIS CHICAGO

Navy Pier, Chicago

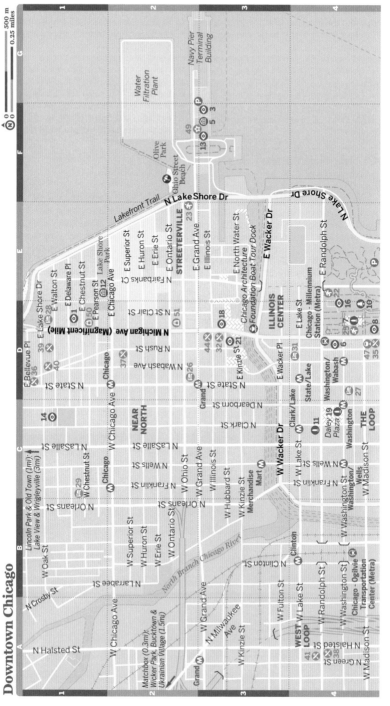

Downtown Chicago

46

N 0
500 m
0.25 miles

Water Filtration Plant

Navy Pier Terminal Building

49
13
P
5 3

Olive Park

Ohio Street Beach

Lakefront Trail

N Lake Shore Dr

N Lake Shore Dr

E Wacker Dr

E Randolph St

STREETERVILLE
23

E Superior St
E Huron St
E Erie St
E Ontario St
E Grand Ave
E Illinois St

E North Water St
N St Clair St
N Fairbanks Ct

Chicago Architecture Foundation Boat Tour Dock

ILLINOIS CENTER

Chicago - Millennium Station (Metra)

E Lake St

22
16
10
8
35
47

E Lake Shore Dr
E Walton St
E Delaware Pl
E Chestnut St
E Pearson St
E Chicago St

E Bellevue Pl

Lake Shore Park

28
1
50
12
51

39
36
40
37
26
44
32
21
18
31
6
27
19
11

N Michigan Ave (Magnificent Mile)

N Rush St
N Wabash Ave
N State St
N Dearborn St
N Clark St

E Kinzie St
E Wacker Dr

Grand
State/Lake
Clark/Lake
Washington/ Wabash
Washington

Daley Plaza

THE LOOP

W Wacker Dr

NEAR NORTH

14

N State St
N LaSalle St
N Wells St
N Franklin St
N Orleans St

W Chicago Ave
W Superior St
W Huron St
W Erie St
W Ontario St
W Grand Ave
W Hubbard St
W Kinzie St

W Lake St
W Washington/ Washington
W Washington St
W Madison St

29

Mart

Merchandise Mart

N LaSalle St
N Chestnut St

Chicago

W Oak St

N Larrabee St
N Crosby St
N Halsted St

W Chicago Ave
W Superior St
W Huron St
W Erie St

Lincoln Park & Old Town (1mi);
Lake View & Wrigleyville (3mi)

Matchbox (0.3mi);
Wicker Park, Bucktown &
Ukrainian Village (1.5mi)

North Branch Chicago River

N Milwaukee Ave

W Fulton St

W Lake St
W Randolph St
W Washington St
W Madison St

WEST LOOP
41
38

N Green St
N Halsted St

N Clinton St
Clinton

Chicago - Ogilvie Transportation Center (Metra)

W Kinzie St
W Grand Ave
W Chicago Ave

N Olive Park

Ohio Street Beach

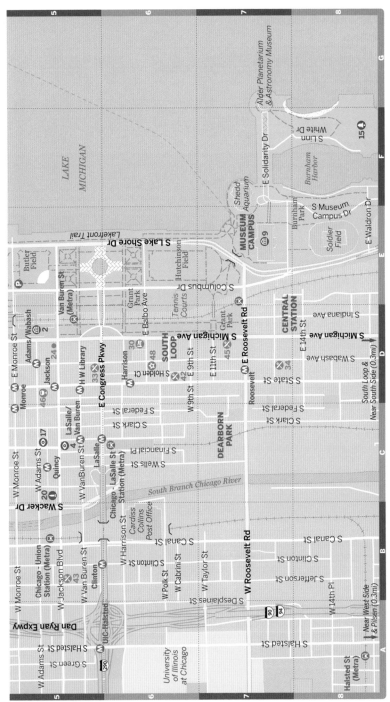

Downtown Chicago

Consider the Museum of Contemporary Art the Art Institute's brash, rebellious sibling, with especially strong minimalist, surrealist and conceptual photography collections, and permanent works by René Magritte, Cindy Sherman and Andy Warhol. Covering art from the 1920s onward, the MCA's collection spans the gamut, with displays arranged to blur the boundaries between painting, sculpture, video and other media. Exhibits change regularly so you never know what you'll see, but you can count on it being offbeat and provocative.

Newberry Library LIBRARY
(☑312-943-9090; www.newberry.org; 60 W Walton St; ⏰galleries 8:15am-5pm Mon, Fri & Sat, to 7:30pm Tue-Thu; Ⓜ Red Line to Chicago) **FREE**
The Newberry's public galleries are for bibliophiles: those who swoon over original Thomas Paine pamphlets about the French Revolution, or get weak-kneed seeing Thomas Jefferson's copy of the *History of the Ex-* *pedition under Captains Lewis and Clark* (with margin notes!). Intriguing exhibits rotate yellowed manuscripts and tattered first editions from the library's extensive collection. The on-site bookstore is tops for Chicago-themed tomes.

◉ Lincoln Park & Old Town

Lincoln Park PARK
(⏰6am-11pm; 🚻; 🚌151) The neighborhood gets its name from this park, Chicago's largest. Its 1200 acres stretch for 6 miles from North Ave north to Diversey Pkwy, where it narrows along the lake and continues on north until the end of Lake Shore Dr. On sunny days locals come out to play in droves, taking advantage of the ponds, paths and playing fields or visiting the zoo and beaches. It's fine spot to while away a morning or afternoon (or both).

Green City Market MARKET

(☑ 773-880-1266; www.greencitymarket.org; 1790 N Clark St; ⊙ 7am-1pm Wed & Sat May-Oct; ⌨ 22) Stands of purple cabbages, red radishes, green asparagus and other bright-hued produce sprawl through Lincoln Park at Chicago's biggest farmers market. Follow your nose to the demonstration tent, where local cooks such as *Top Chef* winner Stephanie Izard prepare dishes – say rice crepes with a mushroom *gastrique* – using market ingredients.

Chicago History Museum MUSEUM

(☑ 312-642-4600; www.chicagohistory.org; 1601 N Clark St; adult/child $16/free; ⊙ 9:30am-4:30pm Mon & Wed-Sat, to 7:30pm Tue, noon-5pm Sun; ⊕; ⌨ 22) Curious about Chicago's storied past? Multimedia displays at this museum cover it all, from the Great Fire to the 1968 Democratic Convention. President Lincoln's deathbed is here, as is the bell worn by Mrs O'Leary's cow. So is the chance to 'become' a Chicago hot dog covered in condiments (in the kids' area, but adults are welcome for the photo op).

◉ Lake View & Wrigleyville

Wrigley Field STADIUM

(www.cubs.com; 1060 W Addison St; Ⓜ Red Line to Addison) Built in 1914 and named for the chewing-gum guy, Wrigley Field is the second-oldest baseball park in the major leagues. It's known for its hand-turned scoreboard, ivy-covered outfield walls and neon sign over the front entrance. It's also known for its team's legendary losing streak. The Cubs (p57) hadn't won a championship since 1908, a cursed dry spell that was unrivaled in US sports. Then in 2016, they triumphed in mythic style. Learn more on 1½-hour tours ($25) of the ballpark, available April through September.

◉ South Loop & Near South Side

Field Museum of Natural History MUSEUM

(☑ 312-922-9410; www.fieldmuseum.org; 1400 S Lake Shore Dr; adult/child $22/15; ⊙ 9am-5pm; ⊕; ⌨ 146, 130) The Field Museum houses some 30 million artifacts and includes everything but the kitchen sink – beetles, mummies, gemstones, Bushman the stuffed ape – all tended by a slew of PhD–wielding scientists, as the Field remains an active research institution. The collection's rock star is Sue, the

largest *Tyrannosaurus rex* yet discovered. She even gets her own gift shop. Special exhibits, such as the 3-D movie, cost extra.

Northerly Island PARK

(1521 S Linn White Dr; ⌨ 146, 130) This hilly, prairie-grassed park has a walking and cycling trail, bird-watching, fishing and an outdoor venue for big-name concerts. It's actually a peninsula, not an island, but the Chicago skyline views are tremendous no matter what you call it. Stop in at the field house, if it's open, for tour information. Bicycles are available at the Divvy bike-share station by the Adler Planetarium. Note that parts of the trail are closed at times due to weather damage.

☞ Tours

Chicago offers loads of tours. Jaunts by boat, foot or bus are popular. They provide a fine introduction to the city, particularly if you're short on time. Bicycle rental companies such as **Bike Chicago** (☑ 312-729-1000; www.bikechicago.com; 239 E Randolph St; bikes per hour/day from $9/30; ⊙ 6:30am-10pm Mon-Fri, from 8am Sat & Sun Jun-Aug, reduced hours rest of year; Ⓜ Brown, Orange, Green, Purple, Pink Line to Washington/Wabash) and **Bobby's Bike Hike** (☑ 312-245-9300; www.bobbysbikehike.com; 540 N Lake Shore Dr; per hour/day from $10/34; ⊙ 8:30am-8pm Mon-Fri, 8am-8pm Sat & Sun Jun-Aug, 9am-7pm Mar-May & Sep-Nov; Ⓜ Red Line to Grand) also run worthy excursions. Outdoor-oriented tours usually operate from April to November only. Many companies offer discounts if you book online.

Chicago Architecture Foundation TOURS

(CAF; ☑ 312-922-3432; www.architecture.org; 224 S Michigan Ave; tours $15-50; Ⓜ Brown, Orange, Green, Purple, Pink Line to Adams) The gold-standard boat tours ($46) sail from the **river dock** (Ⓜ Brown, Orange, Green, Purple, Pink

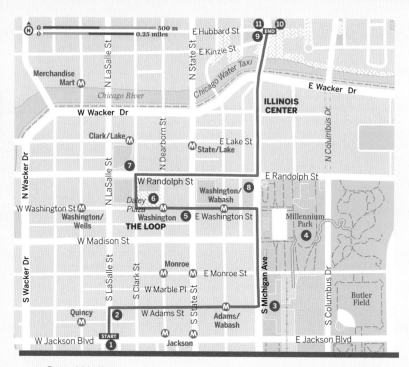

🏃 City Walk
The Loop

START CHICAGO BOARD OF TRADE
FINISH BILLY GOAT TAVERN
LENGTH 3 MILES; ABOUT 2 HOURS

This tour swoops through the Loop, highlighting Chicago's revered art and architecture, with a visit to Al Capone's dentist thrown in for good measure.

Start at the **①Chicago Board of Trade** with its cool art-deco building; that's a giant statue of Ceres, the goddess of agriculture, on top. Step into the nearby **②Rookery** to see Frank Lloyd Wright's handiwork in the atrium.

Head east on Adams St to the **③Art Institute** (p44), one of the city's most-visited attractions. The lion statues out front make a classic keepsake photo. Walk a few blocks north to avant-garde **④Millennium Park** (p44).

Leave the park and head west on Washington St to the **⑤Alise** hotel. It's housed in the Reliance Building, which was the precursor

to modern skyscraper design; Capone's dentist drilled teeth in what's now Room 809. Just to the west, Picasso's abstract **⑥Untitled** sculpture is ensconced in Daley Plaza. Baboon, dog, woman? You decide. Then go north on Clark St to Jean Dubuffet's **⑦Monument with Standing Beast**, another head-scratching sculpture.

Walk east on Randolph St through the theater district. Pop into the **⑧Chicago Cultural Center** to see what free art exhibits or concerts are on. Now go north on Michigan Ave and cross the Chicago River. Just north of the bridge you'll pass the **⑨Wrigley Building**, shining bright and white, and the nearby Gothic, eye-popping **⑩Tribune Tower**.

To finish your tour, visit **⑪Billy Goat Tavern**, a vintage Chicago dive that spawned the Curse of the Cubs after the tavern's owner, Billy Sianis, tried to enter Wrigley Field with his pet goat. The smelly creature was denied entry, so Sianis called down a mighty hex on the baseball team in retaliation. It took them 108 years to break it.

Line to State/Lake) on the southeast side of the Michigan Ave Bridge. The popular Historic Skyscrapers walking tours ($20) leave from the main downtown address. Weekday lunchtime tours ($15) explore individual landmark buildings and meet on-site. CAF sponsors bus, bike and El train tours too. Buy tickets online or at CAF; boat tickets can also be purchased at the dock.

Pilsen Mural Tours　　　WALKING
(📷 773-342-4191; 1½hr tour per group $125) Murals are a traditional Mexican art form, and they're splashed all over Pilsen's buildings. Local artists and activists lead these highly recommended tours that take in the neighborhood's most impressive works. Call to arrange an excursion.

🏄 Activities

Chicago is a rabid sports town, and fans of the pro teams are famously die-hard. It's not all about passively watching sports, though. Chicago offers plenty of places to get active via its city-spanning shoreline, 26 beaches and 580 parks. After a long, cold winter, everyone goes outside to play.

606　　　WALKING, CYCLING
(www.the606.org; ⊙6am-11pm; MBlue Line to Damen) Like NYC's High Line, Chicago's 606 is a similar urban-cool elevated path along an old train track. Bike or stroll past factories, smokestacks, clattering El trains and locals' backyard affairs for 2.7 miles between Wicker Park and Logan Square. It's a fascinating trek through Chicago's socioeconomic strata: moneyed at the east, then becoming more industrial and immigrant to the west. The trail parallels Bloomingdale Ave, with access points every quarter mile.

McCormick Tribune Ice Rink　ICE SKATING
(www.millenniumpark.org; 55 N Michigan Ave; ⊙late Nov-late Feb; MBrown, Orange, Green, Purple, Pink Line to Washington/Wabash) Millennium Park's busy rink is the city's most scenic, tucked between the Bean sculpture and the twinkling lights of Michigan Ave. Admission on the ice is free; skate rental costs $12.

🛏 Sleeping

Accommodations will likely be your biggest expense in Chicago. The best digs are groovy, wired-up boutique hotels, especially those set in architectural landmarks. Several independent hostels have popped up over the past few years in fun, outlying neighbor-

hoods such as Wicker Park and Wrigleyville. Enormous business hotels cater to conventioneers in the Loop and Near North. Lowkey B&Bs are scattered in Wicker Park and Lake View and are often cheaper than hotels.

Fieldhouse Jones　　HOSTEL, HOTEL $
(📷 312-291-9922; www.fieldhousejones.com; 312 W Chestnut St; dm $40-55, r from $150; P❄🐾; MBrown, Purple Line to Chicago) This hostelhotel mashup occupies a vintage, redbrick dairy warehouse. It's great value, drawing a wide range of travelers – global backpackers, families, older couples – for its quality rooms and sociable common areas. There are gender-divided dorms, studios and one- and two-bedroom apartments, all with en suite bathrooms, wi-fi and fun, sporty decor (ie dart board wall art, old trophies etc).

Hollander　　　　HOSTEL $
(📷 872-315-3080; www.thehollander.com; 2022 W North Ave; dm $40-55, r $135-220; P❄🐾; MBlue Line to Damen) The Hollander describes itself as a 'social stay' as opposed to a hostel, and indeed, this revamped, turn-of-the-century warehouse buzzes with the young and perky. Travelers flit in and out of the sunny, shabbychic lobby bar for coffee, laptop musing and bicycle rentals, and they snooze in private rooms and bunk-bed dorms (for four to six people) with polished concrete floors, unvarnished wood-frame beds and other modindustrial decor.

Acme Hotel　　BOUTIQUE HOTEL $$
(📷 312-894-0800; www.acmehotelcompany.com; 15 E Ohio St; r $190-300; P❄@🐾; MRed Line to Grand) Urban bohemians love the Acme for its indie-cool style at (usually) affordable rates. The 130 rooms mix industrial fixtures with retro lamps, mid-century furniture and funky modern art. They're wired up with free wi-fi, good speakers, smart TVs and easy connections to stream your own music and movies. Graffiti, neon and a rock-and-roll elevator embellish the common areas.

Longman & Eagle　　　INN $$
(📷 773-276-7110; www.longmanandeagle.com; 2657 N Kedzie Ave; r $95-200; ❄🐾; MBlue Line to Logan Sq) Check in at the Michelin-starred tavern downstairs and then head to your wood-floored, vintage-stylish accommodations on the floor above. The six rooms aren't particularly soundproof, but after using your whiskey tokens in the bar, you probably won't care. Artwork by local artists decorates each room.

Virgin Hotel
HOTEL $$$

(☎312-940-4400; www.virginhotels.com; 203 N Wabash Ave; r $240-380; P✻@🛜🐾; MBrown, Orange, Green, Purple, Pink Line to State/Lake) Billionaire Richard Branson transformed the 27-story, art-deco Dearborn Bank Building into the first outpost of his cheeky hotel chain. The airy, suite-like rooms have speedy free wi-fi and low-cost minibar items, plus a bed that can double as a work desk. An app controls the thermostat, TV and other electronics. Guests receive earplugs, handy for dulling noise from nearby El trains.

Guesthouse Hotel
BOUTIQUE HOTEL $$$

(☎773-564-9568; www.theguesthousehotel.com; 4872 N Clark St; ste $220-380; P➡✻@🛜🐾; 🚌22, MRed Line to Lawrence) The Guesthouse is comprised of 25 former condominiums that have been converted into huge suites, each with a full kitchen, washer-dryer and private balcony. Choose from a one-, two- or three-bedroom setup. The more expensive suites have a fireplace and extra bathroom. A two- or three-night minimum stay is required, though exceptions are made for last-minute and off-season bookings.

✖ Eating

Chicago has become a chowhound's hot spot. For the most part, restaurants here are reasonably priced and pretension-free, serving masterful food in come-as-you-are environs. You can also fork into a superb range of ethnic eats, especially if you break out of downtown and head for neighborhoods such as Pilsen or Uptown.

✖ The Loop

Most Loop eateries are geared to lunch crowds of office workers. There's not much open after 9pm.

Cafecito
CUBAN $

(☎312-922-2233; www.cafecitochicago.com; 26 E Congress Pkwy; mains $6-10; ⊙7am-9pm Mon-Fri, 10am-6pm Sat & Sun; 🛜; MBrown, Orange, Purple, Pink Line to Library) Attached to the HI-Chicago hostel and perfect for the hungry, thrifty traveler, Cafecito serves killer Cuban sandwiches layered with citrus-garlic-marinated roasted pork and ham. Strong coffee and hearty egg sandwiches make a fine breakfast.

Gage
GASTROPUB $$$

(☎312-372-4243; www.thegagechicago.com; 24 S Michigan Ave; mains $18-36; ⊙11am-9pm Mon, to 11pm Tue-Thu, to midnight Fri, 10am-midnight Sat, 10am-10pm Sun; MBrown, Orange, Green, Purple, Pink Line to Washington/Wabash) This always-hopping gastropub dishes up fanciful grub, from Gouda-topped venison burgers to mussels vindaloo or Guinness-battered fish and chips. The booze rocks too, including a solid whiskey list and small-batch beers that pair with the food.

✖ Near North & Navy Pier

This is where you'll find Chicago's mother lode of restaurants. There's a huge variety, from deep-dish pizza to ritzy seafood.

Giordano's
PIZZA $$

(☎312-951-0747; www.giordanos.com; 730 N Rush St; small pizzas from $16.50; ⊙11am-11pm Sun-Thu, to midnight Fri & Sat; MRed Line to Chicago) Giordano's makes 'stuffed' pizza, a bigger, doughier version of deep dish. It's awesome. If you want a slice of heaven, order the 'special,' a stuffed pie containing sausage, mushroom, green pepper and onions. Each pizza takes 45 minutes to bake.

Purple Pig
MEDITERRANEAN $$

(☎312-464-1744; www.thepurplepigchicago. com; 500 N Michigan Ave; small plates $10-20; ⊙11:30am-midnight Sun-Thu, to 1am Fri & Sat; 🍴; MRed Line to Grand) The Pig's Magnificent Mile location, wide-ranging meat and veggie menu, and late-night serving hours make it a crowd-pleaser. Milk-braised pork shoulder is the hamtastic specialty. Dishes are meant to be shared, and the long list of affordable vinos gets the good times rolling at communal tables both indoors and out. Alas, there are no reservations to help beat the crowds.

✖ Gold Coast

Hendrickx Belgian Bread Crafter
BAKERY $

(☎312-649-6717; www.hendrickxbakery.com; 100 E Walton St; mains $5-12.50; ⊙8am-3:30pm Mon, to 7pm Tue-Sat, 9am-3pm Sun; MRed Line to Chicago) Hiding in a nondescript apartment building, Hendrickx is a local secret. Push open the bright orange door and behold the waffles, white-chocolate bread and dark-chocolate croissants among the flaky, buttery, Belgian treats. The place is tiny, with just a few indoor seats, but in warm weather it sets up tables on the sidewalk. Soups and sandwiches are also available.

Le Colonial FRENCH, VIETNAMESE **$$$**
(☑ 312-255-0088; www.lecolonialchicago.com; 937 N Rush St; mains $22-32; ⊙ 11:30am-3pm & 5-10pm Sun-Thu, to 11pm Fri & Sat; ☑; M Red Line to Chicago) Step into the dark-wood, candlelit room, where ceiling fans swirl lazily and big-leafed palms sway in the breeze, and you'd swear you were in 1920s Saigon. Staff can arrange vegetarian and gluten-free substitutions among the curries and banana-leaf-wrapped fish dishes. If you want spicy, be specific; everything typically comes out mild.

Gibson's STEAK **$$$**
(☑ 312-266-8999; www.gibsonssteakhouse.com; 1028 N Rush St; mains $45-60; ⊙ 11am-midnight; M Red Line to Clark/Division) There is a scene every night at this local original. Politicians, movers, shakers and the shaken-down swirl the famed martinis and compete for prime table space in the buzzing dining room. The rich and beautiful mingle at the bar. As for the meat on the plates, the steaks are as good as they come, and ditto for the ginormous lobsters.

✖ Lincoln Park & Old Town

While mega-high-end restaurants such as Alinea are here, Lincoln Park caters to student tastes too, thanks to the presence of DePaul University. Halsted St, Lincoln Ave and Fullerton Ave are good bets for trendy, flirty eateries. Old Town's eateries are quieter and quainter.

La Fournette BAKERY **$**
(☑ 312-624-9430; www.lafournette.com; 1547 N Wells St; items $3-7; ⊙ 7am-6:30pm Mon-Sat, to 5:30pm Sun; M Brown, Purple Line to Sedgwick) The chef hails from Alsace in France and he fills his narrow, rustic-wood bakery with bright-hued macarons (purple passionfruit, green pistachio, red raspberry-chocolate), cheese-infused breads, crust-crackling baguettes and buttery croissants. They all beg to be devoured on the spot with a cup of locally roasted Intelligentsia coffee. Staff make delicious soups, crepes, quiches and sandwiches with equal French love.

Pequod's Pizza PIZZA **$**
(☑ 773-327-1512; www.pequodspizza.com; 2207 N Clybourn Ave; small pizzas from $12; ⊙ 11am-2am Mon-Sat, to midnight Sun; ☐ 9 to Webster) Like

EAT STREETS
••

Randolph Street, West Loop Chicago's best and brightest chefs cook at downtown's edge.

Clark Street, Andersonville Nouveau Korean, traditional Belgian and Low-country crawfish.

Division Street, Wicker Park Copious sidewalk seating spills out of hip bistros and cafes.

Argyle Street, Uptown Thai and Vietnamese noodle houses steam up this little corridor.

18th Street, Pilsen Mexican bakeries and taquerias mix with hipster cafes and barbecue joints.

the ship in *Moby Dick*, from which this neighborhood restaurant takes its name, Pequod's pan-style (akin to deep dish) pizza is a thing of legend – head and shoulders above chain competitors because of its caramelized cheese, generous toppings and sweetly flavored sauce. Neon beer signs glow from the walls, and Blackhawks jerseys hang from the ceiling in the affably rugged interior.

Wait times can be long, but you can pass the time drinking at the WhaleTale bar one door away; Pequod's will page you when your table is ready.

Twin Anchors BARBECUE **$$**
(☑ 312-266-1616; www.twinanchorsribs.com; 1655 N Sedgwick St; mains $17-28; ⊙ 5-10:30pm Mon-Thu, to midnight Fri, noon-midnight Sat, noon-10:30pm Sun; M Brown, Purple Line to Sedgwick) Twin Anchors is synonymous with ribs – smoky, tangy-sauced baby backs in this case. The meat drops from the ribs as soon as you lift them. The restaurant doesn't take reservations, so you'll have to wait outside or around the neon-lit 1950s bar, which sets the tone for the place. An almost-all-Sinatra jukebox completes the supper-club ambience.

Alinea GASTRONOMY **$$$**
(☑ 312-867-0110; www.alinearestaurant.com; 1723 N Halsted St; 10-/16-course menu from $165/285; ⊙ 5-10pm Wed-Sun; M Red Line to North/Clybourn) One of the world's best restaurants, with three Michelin stars, Alinea brings on multiple courses of molecular gastronomy. Dishes may emanate from a centrifuge or

Baseball game at Wrigley Field (p49)

be pressed into a capsule, à la duck served with a 'pillow of lavender air.' There are no reservations; instead Alinea sells tickets two to three months in advance via its website. Check Twitter (@Alinea) for any last-minute seats.

✖ Lake View & Wrigleyville

Good-time midrange places for vegetarians and global food lovers fill the neighborhood. Clark, Halsted and Southport are fertile grazing streets.

Crisp   KOREAN $

(☑773-697-7610; www.crisponline.com; 2940 N Broadway; mains $9-13; ⊙11:30am-9pm; Ⓜ Brown, Purple Line to Wellington) Music pours from the stereo while delicious Korean fusions arrive from the kitchen at this cheerful cafe. The 'Bad Boy Buddha' bowl, a variation on *bi bim bop* (mixed vegetables with rice), is one of the best healthy lunches in town. Crisp's fried chicken (especially the 'Seoul Sassy' with its savory soy-ginger sauce) also wows the casual crowd.

mfk   SPANISH $$

(☑773-857-2540; www.mfkrestaurant.com; 432 W Diversey Pkwy; small plates $10-18; ⊙5-10pm Mon & Tue, noon-10pm Wed & Thu, to midnight Fri & Sat, to 10pm Sun; ⊒22) In mfk's teeny space it feels like you're having a romantic meal in Spain, with the sea lapping just outside the door. Dig into crunchy prawn heads,

garlicky octopus and veal meatballs amid the whitewashed walls and decorative tiles. Sunny cocktails and a wine list dominated by whites and rosés add to the goodness.

The restaurant is named after renowned food writer MFK Fisher, a foodie well before her time.

✖ South Loop & Near South Side

Options are a bit sparse in the South Loop. Cheap eats for students predominate. They give way to Chinatown's abundant flavors as you move southwest.

Lou Malnati's   PIZZA $

(☑312-786-1000; www.loumalnatis.com; 805 S State St; small pizzas from $13; ⊙11am-11pm Sun-Thu, to midnight Fri & Sat; Ⓜ Red Line to Harrison) Lou Malnati's is one of the city's premier deep-dish pizza makers. In fact, it claims to have invented the gooey behemoth (though that's a matter of never-ending dispute). Not in dispute: the deliciousness of Malnati's famed butter crust. Gluten-free diners can opt for the sausage crust (it's literally just meat, no dough). The restaurant has outlets citywide.

Qing Xiang Yuan Dumplings   DUMPLINGS $

(☑312-799-1118; www.qxydumplings.com; 2002 S Wentworth Ave, Ste 103; mains $8-12; ⊙11am-11pm; Ⓜ Red Line to Cermak-Chinatown) The name doesn't lie: it's all about dumplings in this bright room under bamboo lanterns. They come steamed by the dozen, with fillings such as lamb and coriander, ground pork and cabbage, sea whelk and leek, and some 30 other types. Bite into one and a hot shot of flavor erupts in your mouth. Located upstairs in the Richland Center food court.

Yolk BREAKFAST **$**

(☎312-789-9655; www.eatyolk.com; 1120 S Michigan Ave; mains $10-14; ⊙6am-3pm Mon-Fri, 7am-3pm Sat & Sun; 👪; MRed, Orange, Green Line to Roosevelt) This cheerful diner is worth the long wait – you'll dig into the best traditional breakfast in the South Loop. The omelets include lots of healthy options (the Iron Man is made from egg whites and comes loaded with veggies and avocado), and sweets lovers have stacks of choices, including cinnamon-roll French toast and peach-cobbler crepes drenched in syrup.

Flo & Santos PUB FOOD **$$**

(☎312-566-9817; www.floandsantos.com; 1310 S Wabash Ave; mains $12-19; ⊙11:30am-11pm Sun-Thu, to midnight Fri & Sat; MRed, Orange, Green Line to Roosevelt) This South Loop neighborhood pub is known for its tavern-style pizza (with wafer-thin crust and sweet sauce) and its Polish dishes (such as pierogi and potato pancakes). Eat in the warm, exposed-brick interior or in the outdoor beer garden at umbrella-shaded picnic tables under strands of winking lights.

Mercat a la Planxa SPANISH **$$$**

(☎312-765-0524; www.mercatchicago.com; 638 S Michigan Ave; tapas $10-17, tasting menus from $65; ⊙11am-10pm Mon-Thu, to 11pm Fri, 10am-11pm Sat, 10am-10pm Sun; MRed Line to Harrison) This Barcelona-style tapas and seafood restaurant buzzes in an enormous, convivial room where light streams in through the floor-to-ceiling windows. It cooks all the specialties of Catalonia and stokes a festive atmosphere, enhanced by copious quantities of *cava* (sparkling wine) and sangria. It's located in the beaux-arts **Blackstone Hotel** (☎312-447-0955; www.blackstonerenaissance.com; 636 S Michigan Ave; r $199-319; P❄@📶🐾; MRed Line to Harrison).

Near West Side & Pilsen

The West Loop booms with celebrity-chef restaurants. Stroll along W Randolph St and W Fulton Market and take your pick. Greektown extends along S Halsted St, Little Italy along Taylor St. Mexican taquerias meet hipster hangouts along 18th St in Pilsen.

Pleasant House Pub PUB FOOD **$**

(☎773-523-7437; www.facebook.com/pleasanthousepub; 2119 S Halsted St; mains $8-10; ⊙7am-10pm Tue-Thu, to midnight Fri, 10am-midnight Sat, to 10pm Sun; 📶; 🚌8) Follow your nose to Pleasant House, which bakes tall, fluffy, savory pies. Daily flavors include chicken and chutney, steak and ale, or kale and mushroom, made with produce the chefs grow themselves. The pub also serves its own beers (brewed off-site) to accompany the food. Friday is a good day to visit, when there's a fish fry.

Lou Mitchell's BREAKFAST **$**

(☎312-939-3111; www.loumitchellsrestaurant.com; 565 W Jackson Blvd; mains $9-14; ⊙5:30am-3pm Mon, to 4pm Tue-Fri, 7am-4pm Sat, to 3pm Sun; 👪; MBlue Line to Clinton) A relic of Route 66, Lou's brings in elbow-to-elbow locals and tourists for breakfast. The old-school waitresses deliver fluffy omelets that hang off the plate and thick-cut French toast with a jug of syrup. They call you 'honey' and fill your coffee cup endlessly. There's often a queue to get in, but free doughnut holes and Milk Duds help ease the wait.

Little Goat DINER **$$**

(☎312-888-3455; www.littlegoatchicago.com; 820 W Randolph St; mains $10-19; ⊙7am-10pm Sun-Thu, to midnight Fri & Sat; 📶🍷; MGreen, Pink Line to Morgan) *Top Chef* winner Stephanie Izard opened this diner for the foodie masses across the street from her ever-booked main restaurant, **Girl & the Goat** (☎312-492-6262; www.girlandthegoat.com; 809 W Randolph St; small plates $9-16; ⊙4:30-11pm Sun-Thu, to midnight Fri & Sat; 🍷; MGreen, Pink Line to Morgan). Scooch into a vintage booth and order off the all-day breakfast menu. Better yet, try lunch and dinner favorites such as the goat sloppy joe with rosemary slaw or pork belly on scallion pancakes. Izard's flavor combinations rule.

Wicker Park, Bucktown & Ukrainian Village

Trendy restaurants open almost every day, with many serving nouveau comfort food. Division St is a bountiful vein of snazzy bistros and pubs that have sidewalk seating.

Irazu
LATIN AMERICAN $

(☑773-252-5687; www.irazuchicago.com; 1865 N Milwaukee Ave; mains $11-15; ⊘11:30am-9:30pm Mon-Sat; Ⓜ Blue Line to Western) Chicago's unassuming lone Costa Rican eatery turns out burritos bursting with chicken, black beans and fresh avocado, and sandwiches dressed in a heavenly, spicy-sweet vegetable sauce. Wash them down with an *avena* (a slurpable oatmeal milkshake). For breakfast, the *arroz con huevos* (peppery eggs scrambled into rice) relieves hangovers. Irazu is BYOB with no corkage fee. Cash only.

Dove's Luncheonette
TEX-MEX $$

(☑773-645-4060; www.doveschicago.com; 1545 N Damen Ave; mains $13-19; ⊘9am-9pm Mon-Thu, 8am-10pm Fri & Sat, 8am-9pm Sun; Ⓜ Blue Line to Damen) Grab a seat at the retro counter for Tex-Mex plates of pork-shoulder posole and shrimp-stuffed sweet-corn tamales. Dessert? It's pie, of course – maybe lemon cream or peach jalapeno, depending on what staff have baked that day. Soul music spins on a record player, tequila flows from the 70 bottles rattling behind the bar, and presto: all is right in the world.

Drinking & Nightlife

Chicagoans love to hang out in drinking establishments. Blame it on the long winter, when folks need to huddle together somewhere warm. Blame it on summer, when sunny days make beer gardens and sidewalk patios so splendid. Whatever the reason, drinking is a widely cherished civic pastime.

Berghoff
BAR

(☑312-427-3170; www.theberghoff.com; 17 W Adams St; ⊘11am-9pm Mon-Fri, 11:30am-9pm Sat; Ⓜ Blue, Red Line to Jackson) The Berghoff dates from 1898 and was the first spot in town to serve a legal drink after Prohibition (ask to see the liquor license stamped '#1'). Little has changed around the antique wood bar since then. Belly up for frosty mugs of the house-brand beer and order sauerbraten, schnitzel and other old-world classics from the adjoining German restaurant.

Signature Lounge
LOUNGE

(www.signatureroom.com; 875 N Michigan Ave, John Hancock Center, 96th fl; ⊘11am-12:30am Sun-Thu, to 1:30am Fri & Sat; Ⓜ Red Line to Chicago) Take the elevator to the 96th floor of the John Hancock Center and order a beverage while looking out over the city from some 1000ft up in the sky. It's particularly gape-worthy at night. Ladies: don't miss the bathroom view.

Old Town Ale House
BAR

(☑312-944-7020; www.theoldtownalehouse.com; 219 W North Ave; ⊘3pm-4am Mon-Fri, from noon Sat & Sun; Ⓜ Brown, Purple Line to Sedgwick) Located near the Second City comedy club and the scene of late-night musings since the 1960s, this unpretentious neighborhood favorite lets you mingle with beautiful people and grizzled regulars, seated pint by pint under the nude-politician paintings. Classic jazz on the jukebox provides the soundtrack for the jovial goings-on. Cash only.

Matchbox
BAR

(☑312-666-9292; 770 N Milwaukee Ave; ⊘4pm-2am Mon-Thu, from 3pm Fri-Sun; Ⓜ Blue Line to Chicago) Lawyers, artists and bums all squeeze in for retro cocktails. It's as small as – you got it – a matchbox, with about 10 bar stools; everyone else stands against the back wall. Barkeeps make the drinks from scratch. Favorites include the pisco sour and the ginger gimlet, ladled from an amber vat of homemade ginger-infused vodka.

Spoke & Bird
CAFE

(www.spokeandbird.com; 205 E 18th St; ⊘7am-6pm; ☎; 🖵1) The South Loop has been begging for a leafy patio like the one at Spoke & Bird. Bonus: it's surrounded by several cool old manors in the Prairie Avenue Historic District. Relax with a locally made brew and nifty cafe fare such as the sweet parsnip muffin or lamb barbecue sandwich.

Revolution Brewing
BREWERY

(☑773-227-2739; www.revbrew.com; 2323 N Milwaukee Ave; ⊘11am-1am Mon-Fri, 10am-1am Sat, 10am-11pm Sun; Ⓜ Blue Line to California) Raise your fist to Revolution, a big, buzzy, industrial-chic brewpub that fills glasses with heady beers such as the Eugene porter and hopped-up Anti-Hero IPA. The brewmaster here led the way for Chicago's huge craft beer scene, and his suds are top notch. The haute pub grub includes a pork belly and egg sandwich and bacon-fat popcorn with fried sage.

Coq d'Or
LOUNGE

(☑312-932-4623; 140 E Walton St; ⊘11am-1am Sun-Thu, to 2am Fri & Sat; Ⓜ Red Line to Chicago) This classy joint in the **Drake Hotel** (☑312-787-2200; www.thedrakehotel.com; r $230-360; Ⓟ✳@☎) opened the day after Prohibition was repealed. It offers a taste of old Chicago: burgundy-colored leather booths, snazzy bartenders and bejeweled women in furs sipping Manhattans. A piano player starts tinkling the ivories around 9pm on weekends.

Cindy's
BAR

(📞312-792-3502; www.cindysrooftop.com; 12 S Michigan Ave; ⊙11am-1am Mon-Fri, 10am-2am Sat, to midnight Sun; Ⓜ Brown, Orange, Green, Purple, Pink Line to Washington/Wabash) Cindy's unfurls awesome views of Millennium Park and the lake from atop the Chicago Athletic Association Hotel. Sit at one of the long wood tables under twinkling lights and sip snazzy cocktails with ingredients such as mugolio pine sap. Alas, everyone wants in on the action, so try to come early to avoid having to wait for a seat.

Queen Mary
BAR

(www.queenmarytavern.com; 2125 W Division St; ⊙5pm-2am Sun-Fri, to 3am Sat; Ⓜ Blue Line to Division) Making waves when it opened in Wicker Park in 2015 in a sea of sports bars, Queen Mary is a neighborhood tavern inspired by the British Royal Navy. It's named after building owner Mary Kafka, who, alongside her husband, ran a Polish dive bar in the same spot during the 1970s.

Violet Hour
COCKTAIL BAR

(📞773-252-1500; www.theviolethour.com; 1520 N Damen Ave; ⊙6pm-2am Sun-Fri, to 3am Sat; Ⓜ Blue Line to Damen) This nouveau speakeasy isn't marked, so look for the mural-slathered, wood-paneled building and the door topped by a yellow lightbulb. Inside, velvet drapes provide the backdrop to elaborately engineered cocktails that the Beard Awards deemed best in the US. The Pajama Boy (bourbon and pear brandy) shows why. As highbrow as it sounds, Violet Hour is welcoming and accessible.

☆ Entertainment

Finding something to do in Chicago on any given night is effortless, and the spectrum of entertainment that's available in every price range is overwhelming. Just flip through the city's news weekly, the *Reader,* with its pages of theater openings and concert announcements, and Chicagoans' insatiable appetite for nocturnal amusement becomes apparent.

Chicago Cubs
BASEBALL

(📞800-843-2827; www.cubs.com; 1060 W Addison St; Ⓜ Red Line to Addison) The beloved Cubs play at old-time Wrigley Field. For 108 years they didn't win a championship – the longest losing streak in US sports history – but in 2016 the team broke the curse. Games

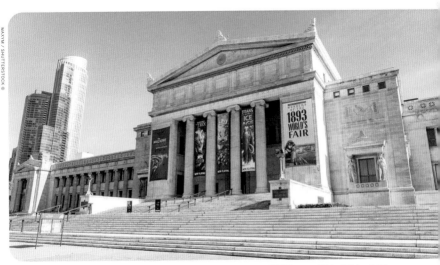

Field Museum of Natural History (p49)

are always packed. Ticket prices vary, but in general you'll be hard-pressed to get in for under $40. The popular bleacher seats cost around $55 or so.

Grant Park Orchestra
CLASSICAL MUSIC

(☑312-742-7638;www.grantparkmusicfestival.com; Pritzker Pavilion, Millennium Park; ⏰6:30pm Wed & Fri, 7:30pm Sat mid-Jun–mid-Aug; Ⓜ Brown, Orange, Green, Purple, Pink Line to Washington/Wabash) It's a summertime must-do. The Grant Park Orchestra – composed of top-notch musicians from symphonies worldwide – puts on free classical concerts at Millennium Park's Pritzker Pavilion (p44). Patrons bring lawn chairs, blankets, wine and picnic fixings to set the scene as the sun dips, the skyscraper lights flicker on and glorious music fills the night air.

iO Theater
COMEDY

(☑312-929-2401;   www.ioimprov.com/chicago; 1501 N Kingsbury St; tickets $5-16; Ⓜ Red Line to North/Clybourn) One of Chicago's top-tier improv houses, iO is a bit edgier (and cheaper) than its competition, with four stages hosting bawdy shows nightly. Two bars and a beer garden add to the fun. The Improvised Shakespeare Company is awesome; catch them if you can.

Metro
LIVE MUSIC

(☑773-549-4140; www.metrochicago.com; 3730 N Clark St; ⏰box office noon-6pm Mon, to 8pm Tue-Sat; Ⓜ Red Line to Addison) For more than three decades, the Metro has been synonymous with loud rock. Sonic Youth and the Ramones in the '80s. Nirvana and Jane's Addiction in the '90s. White Stripes and the Killers in the new millennium. Each night prepare to hear new noise by three or four bands who may well be teetering on the verge of stardom.

Second City
COMEDY

(☑312-337-3992; www.secondcity.com; 1616 N Wells St; tickets $29-36; Ⓜ Brown, Purple Line to Sedgwick) Bill Murray, Stephen Colbert, Tina Fey and more honed their wit at this slick venue where shows take place nightly. The Mainstage and ETC stage host sketch revues (with an improv scene thrown in); they're similar in price and quality. If you turn up around 10pm (on any night except Friday and Saturday) you can have yourself a bargain and watch the comics improvise a set for free.

Steppenwolf Theatre
THEATER

(☑312-335-1650; www.steppenwolf.org; 1650 N Halsted St; Ⓜ Red Line to North/Clybourn) Steppenwolf is Chicago's top stage for quality, provocative theater productions. The Hollywood-heavy ensemble includes Gary Sinise, John Malkovich, Martha Plimpton, Gary Cole, Joan Allen and Tracy Letts. A money-saving tip: the box office releases 20 tickets for $20 for each day's shows; they go on sale at 11am Monday to Saturday and at 1pm Sunday, and are available by phone.

Hideout
LIVE MUSIC

(☑773-227-4433; www.hideoutchicago.com; 1354 W Wabansia Ave; tickets $5-15; ⏰5pm-2am Mon & Tue, from 4pm Wed-Fri, 7pm-3am Sat, hours vary Sun; ⧉72) Hidden behind a factory at the edge of Bucktown, this two-room lodge of indie rock and alt-country is well worth seeking out. The owners have nursed an outsider, underground vibe, and the place feels like your grandma's rumpus room. Music and other events (talk shows, literary readings etc) take place nightly.

Buddy Guy's Legends
BLUES

(☑312-427-1190; www.buddyguy.com; 700 S Wabash Ave; tickets Sun-Thu $10, Fri & Sat $20; ⏰5pm-2am Mon & Tue, from 11am Wed-Fri, noon-3am Sat, to 2am Sun; Ⓜ Red Line to Harrison) Top local and national acts wail on the stage of local icon Buddy Guy. The man himself usually plugs in his axe for a series of shows in January (tickets go on sale in November). The location is a bit rough around the edges, but the acts are consistently excellent.

🛍 Shopping

Music is big. Independent record stores flood Chicago's neighborhoods, supported by the thriving live-music scene in town. Vinyl geeks will find heaps of stacks to flip through. Vintage and thrift fashions are another claim to fame. Folks here don't throw out their old bowling shirts, pillbox hats, faux-fur coats and costume jewelry. Instead, they deposit used duds at vintage or second-hand stores, of which there are heaps. Art- and architecture-related items are another Chicago specialty.

Reckless Records
MUSIC

(☑773-235-3727; www.reckless.com; 1379 N Milwaukee Ave; ⏰10am-10pm Mon-Sat, to 8pm Sun; Ⓜ Blue Line to Damen) Chicago's best indie-rock record and CD emporium allows you to listen to everything before you buy.

CHICAGO'S TOP EVENTS

St Patrick's Day Parade (www.chicagostpatricksdayparade.org; ☺ mid-Mar) The local plumbers union dyes the Chicago River shamrock green; a big parade follows downtown in Grant Park. Held the Saturday before March 17.

Chicago Blues Festival (www.chicagobluesfestival.us; ☺ mid-Jun) The biggest free blues fest in the world, with three days of the music that made Chicago famous. Held in Millennium Park.

Pride Parade (http://chicagopride.gopride.com; ☺ late Jun) On the last Sunday in June, colorful floats and risqué revelers pack Halsted St in Boystown. It's the LGBTIQ+ community's main event, and more than 800,000 people come to the party.

Lollapalooza (www.lollapalooza.com; day pass $120; ☺ early Aug) Up to 170 bands spill off eight stages at Grant Park's four-day mega-gig.

It's certainly the place to get your finger on the pulse of the local, au courant underground scene. There's plenty of elbow room in the big, sunny space, which makes for happy hunting through the new and used bins. Reasonable prices too.

Garrett Popcorn
FOOD

(☏ 312-944-2630; www.garrettpopcorn.com; 625 N Michigan Ave; ☺ 10am-8pm Mon-Thu, to 10pm Fri & Sat, to 7pm Sun; Ⓜ Red Line to Grand) Like lemmings drawn to a cliff, people form long lines outside this store on the Mag Mile. Granted, the caramel corn is heavenly and the cheese popcorn decadent, but is it worth waiting in the whipping snow for a chance to buy some? Actually, it is. Buy the Garrett Mix, which combines the two flavors. The entrance is on Ontario St.

American Girl Place
TOYS

(☏ 877-247-5223; www.americangirl.com; 835 N Michigan Ave, Water Tower Place; ☺ 10am-8pm Mon-Thu, to 9pm Fri, 9am-9pm Sat, 9am-6pm Sun; ♿; Ⓜ Red Line to Chicago) This is not your mother's doll shop; it's an *experience*. Here dolls are treated as real people: the 'hospital' carts them away in wheelchairs for repairs, and the cafe seats the dolls as part of the family during tea service. While there are American Girl stores in many cities, this flagship remains the largest and busiest.

Quimby's
BOOKS

(☏ 773-342-0910; www.quimbys.com; 1854 W North Ave; ☺ noon-9pm Mon-Thu, to 10pm Fri, 11am-10pm Sat, noon-7pm Sun; Ⓜ Blue Line to Damen) The epicenter of Chicago's comic and zine worlds, Quimby's is one of the linchpins of underground culture in the city. Here you

can find everything from crayon-powered punk-rock manifestos to slickly produced graphic novels. It's a groovy place for cheeky literary souvenirs and bizarro readings.

Dave's Records
MUSIC

(☏ 773-929-6325; www.davesrecordschicago.com; 2604 N Clark St; ☺ 11am-8pm Mon-Sat, noon-7pm Sun; Ⓜ Brown, Purple Line to Diversey) *Rolling Stone* magazine picked Dave's as one of the nation's best record stores. It has an 'all vinyl, all the time' mantra, meaning crate diggers will be in their element flipping through the stacks of rock, jazz, blues, folk and house. Dave himself usually mans the counter, where you'll find a slew of 25-cent cheapie records for sale.

❶ Getting Around

The El (a system of elevated and subway trains) is the main way to get around. Buses are also useful. Buy a day pass for $10 at El stations. The Chicago Transit Authority (www.transitchicago.com) runs the transport system.

Train El trains are fast, frequent and ubiquitous. Red and Blue Lines operate 24/7; others between 4am and 1am.

Bus Buses cover areas that the El misses. Most run at least from early morning until 10pm; some go later. Some don't run on weekends.

Taxi Easy to find downtown, north to Andersonville and west to Wicker Park/Bucktown. But costly.

Boat Water taxis travel along the river and lakefront and offer a fun way to reach the Museum Campus or Chinatown.

Bicycle Abundant rental shops and the Divvy bike-share program make cycling a doable option.

Lincoln Home & Visitor Center, Springfield

Springfield

The small state capital has a serious obsession with Abraham Lincoln, who practiced law here from 1837 to 1861. Many of the attractions are walkable downtown and cost little or nothing.

◎ Sights

Lincoln Home & Visitor Center   HISTORIC SITE
(☑217-492-4150; www.nps.gov/liho; 426 S 7th St; ⊗8:30am-5pm) **FREE** Start at the National Park Service visitor center, where you must pick up a ticket to enter Lincoln's 12-room abode, located directly across the street. You can then walk through the house where Abe and Mary Lincoln lived from 1844 until they moved to the White House in 1861; rangers are stationed throughout to provide background information and answer questions.

**Lincoln Presidential
Library & Museum**   MUSEUM
(☑217-558-8844; www.illinois.gov/alplm; 212 N 6th St; adult/child $15/6; ⊗9am-5pm; 🖼) This museum contains the most complete Lincoln collection in the world. Real-deal artifacts like Abe's shaving mirror and briefcase join whiz-bang exhibits and Disney-esque holograms that keep the kids agog.

🛏 Sleeping

Springfield has lots of chain hotels aimed at business travelers. The lodgings aren't terribly charismatic, but they have all the modern conveniences. Prices can be high, depending on what's happening in and around the Capitol.

Inn at 835   B&B $$
(☑217-523-4466; www.innat835.com; 835 S 2nd St; r $135-205; P❄🛜) The historic, arts-and-crafts-style manor offers 11 rooms of the four-post bed, claw-foot bathtub variety.

State House Inn   HOTEL $$
(☑217-528-5100; www.thestatehouseinn.com; 101 E Adams St; r $120-165; P❄@🛜) It looks concrete-drab outside, but inside the State House shows its style. Comfy beds and large baths fill the rooms; a retro bar fills the lobby. Hot breakfast included.

🍴 Eating

Restaurants cluster in the small downtown between the old Capitol and new Capitol buildings. Most are sandwich and burger joints or more upscale steak and seafood spots where politicians hobnob. Keep an eye out for the horseshoe, a local specialty that consists of fried meat, french fries and melted cheese served in an open-faced sandwich.

Cozy Dog Drive In
AMERICAN $

(217-525-1992; www.cozydogdrivein.com; 2935 S 6th St; mains $2-5; ⊙8am-8pm Mon-Sat) This Route 66 legend – the reputed birthplace of the corn dog! – has memorabilia and souvenirs in addition to the deeply fried main course on a stick.

D'Arcy's Pint
PUB FOOD $

(217-492-8800; www.darcyspintonline.com; 661 W Stanford Ave; mains $9-14; ⊙11am-10pm Mon-Thu, to 11pm Fri & Sat, noon-5:30pm Sun) D'Arcy's piles up Springfield's best 'horseshoe,' a local sandwich of fried meat on toasted bread, mounded with french fries and smothered in melted cheese. There's also a full menu of Irish dishes, including fried oysters and shepherd's pie.

🍷 Drinking

Downtown offers plenty of casual saloons, sports bars and Irish pubs to get a craft beer or cocktail; browse around 5th and Monroe Sts.

Obed & Isaac's
MICROBREWERY

(217-670-0627; www.obedandisaacs.com; 500 S 6th St; ⊙11am-11:30pm) Set in a rambling, 150-year-old mansion by Abe Lincoln's home, Obed & Isaac's offers a maze of sunny rooms to drink its wildly changing menu of ales and stouts brewed onsite. Flights let you sample freely, while the menu of elevated bar (try the ponyshoe) food helps soak up the alcohol. An outdoor bar, patio and bocce courts await in summer.

☆ Entertainment

Route 66 Drive In
CINEMA

(217-698-0066; www.route66-drivein.com; 1700 Recreation Dr; adult/child $7.50/5; ⊙nightly Jun-Aug, weekends mid-Apr–May & Sep) Screens first-run flicks under the stars.

ⓘ Information

Springfield Convention & Visitors Bureau (www.visitspringfieldillinois.com) Produces a useful visitors' guide.

Missouri to Oklahoma

Endless horizons, beguiling open spaces and soaring bluffs.

MISSOURI

The most populated state in the Plains, Missouri likes to mix things up, serving visitors ample portions of both sophisticated city life and down-home country sights. St Louis and Kansas City are the region's most interesting cities, and each is a destination in its own right. But, with more forest and less farm field than neighboring states, Missouri also cradles plenty of wild places and wide-open spaces, most notably the rolling Ozark Mountains, where the winding valleys invite adventurous exploration or just some laid-back meandering behind the steering wheel. Maybe you'll find an adventure worthy of Hannibal native Mark Twain as you wander the state.

St Louis

Slide into St Louis and revel in the unique vibe of the largest city in the Great Plains. Beer, bowling and baseball are some of the top attractions, but history and culture, much of it linked to the Mississippi River, are a vital part of the fabric. And, of course, there's the iconic Gateway Arch that you have seen in a million pictures; it's even more impressive in reality. Many music

legends, including Scott Joplin, Chuck Berry, Tina Turner and Miles Davis, got their start here and jammin' live-music venues keep the flame burning.

☉ Sights

**Gateway Arch & Jefferson
National Expansion Memorial** MONUMENT
(☑314-655-1700; www.gatewayarch.com; tram ride adult/child $13/10; ☉8am-10pm Jun-Aug, 9am-6pm Sep-May, last tram 1hr before closing; ☑) As a symbol for St Louis, the Arch has soared above any expectations its backers could have had in 1965 when it opened. The centerpiece of the Jefferson National Expansion Memorial (a National Park Service property), the silvery, shimmering Gateway Arch is the Great Plains' own Eiffel Tower. It stands 630ft high and symbolizes St Louis' historical role as 'Gateway to the West.' The tram ride takes you to the tight confines at the top.

Forest Park PARK
(☑314-367-7275; www.forestparkforever.org; bounded by Lindell Blvd, Kingshighway Blvd & I-64; ☉6am-10pm) New York City may have Central Park, but St Louis has the bigger (by 528 acres) Forest Park. The superb, 1371-acre spread was the setting of the 1904

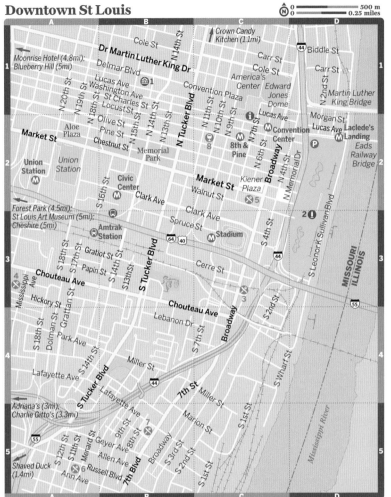

World's Fair. It's a beautiful place to escape to for a few hours and is dotted with attractions, many of which are free. Two walkable neighborhoods, the Loop and Central West End, are close.

City Museum   MUSEUM
(www.citymuseum.org; 701 N 15th St; $12, Ferris wheel $5; ⊘9am-5pm Mon-Thu, to midnight Fri & Sat, 11am-5pm Sun; ⊞) Possibly the wildest highlight to any visit to St Louis is this frivolous, frilly fun house in a vast old shoe factory. The **Museum of Mirth, Mystery & Mayhem** sets the tone. Run, jump and explore all manner of exhibits, including a

seven-story slide. The summer-only roof-top Ferris wheel offers grand views across St Louis.

St Louis Art Museum
MUSEUM

(www.slam.org; 1 Fine Arts Dr; ⊘10am-5pm Tue-Thu, Sat & Sun, to 9pm Fri) **FREE** This grand beaux-arts palace (with a striking modern wing) was originally built for the World's Fair. Now housing this storied institution, its collection spans time and styles, and includes a variety of household names from Picasso to Van Gogh and Warhol. The Grace Taylor Broughton Sculpture Garden opened in 2015.

🛏 Sleeping

Most midrange and upscale chains have a hotel near the Gateway Arch (p62) in Downtown. Indie cheapies are thin on the ground in interesting areas, but you'll find plenty near the airport and you can ride the MetroLink light rail into the city. Clayton on I-170 (exit 1F) also has rail access and a cluster of chains.

Cheshire
HOTEL $$

(☑314-647-7300; www.cheshirestl.com; 6300 Clayton Rd; r $150-250; P❊🎧🐾) This upscale inn situated near Forest Park (p62) oozes character, from its stained-glass windows to the all-encompassing British literary theme. The hodgepodge collection of artworks, antique furnishings and (occasionally frightening) taxidermy are sure to delight.

Moonrise Hotel
BOUTIQUE HOTEL $$

(☑314-721-1111; www.moonrisehotel.com; 6177 Delmar Blvd; r $170-450; P❊🎧🐾) The stylish eight-story Moonrise has a high profile amid the high energy of the Loop neighborhood. Its 125 rooms sport a lunar motif, but are grounded enough to slow things down to comfy.

🍴 Eating

St Louis boasts the region's most diverse selection of food, from the Irish pubs of Soulard to the Asian restaurants along South Grand. Don't leave town without sampling the city's unique approach to Italian-American cuisine in the Hill. The magazine and website *Sauce* (www.saucemagazine.com) is full of great reviews.

Crown Candy Kitchen
CAFE $

(☑314-621-9650; www.crowncandykitchen.net; 1401 St Louis Ave; mains $5-10; ⊘10:30am-8pm Mon-Thu, to 9pm Fri & Sat; 🚼) An authentic family run soda fountain that's been making families smile since 1913. Malts (hot fudge, yum!) come with spoons, the floats, well, float, and you can try the famous BLT. Homemade candies top it off. It's an oasis in the struggling North St Louis neighborhood.

Adriana's
ITALIAN $

(☑314-773-3833; www.adrianasonthehill.com; 5101 Shaw Ave; mains $5-10; ⊘10:30am-3pm Mon-Sat) Redolent of herbs, this family-owned Italian deli serves up fresh salads and sandwiches (get the meaty Hill Boy) to ravenous lunching crowds. Expect lines.

ST LOUIS SPECIALTIES

Toasted ravioli They're filled with meat, coated in breadcrumbs, then deep-fried. Practically every restaurant on the Hill serves them, most notably Charlie Gitto's (☑314-772-8898; www.charliegittos.com; 5226 Shaw Ave; mains $16-30; ⊘5-10pm Mon-Thu, to 11pm Fri & Sat, 4-9pm Sun; P).

St Louis pizza The thin-crusted, square-cut pizzas here are really addictive. They're made with Provel cheese, a locally beloved gooey concoction of processed cheddar, Swiss and provolone. Local chain Imo's (☑314-641-8899; www.imospizza.com; 1 S Broadway; large pizzas from $16; ⊘11am-7pm Mon-Sat), with over 70 locations across the metro area, bakes 'the square beyond compare,' or get your pizza with Provel at the popular Joanie's Pizzeria (www.joanies.com; 2101 Menard St; mains $10-15; ⊘11am-1am Mon-Sat, to midnight Sun).

Frozen custard Don't dare leave town without licking yourself silly on this super-creamy ice-cream-like treat at historic Ted Drewes (☑314-481-2652; www.teddrewes.com; 6726 Chippewa St; cones $2-6; ⊘11am-11pm Feb-Dec), southwest of the city center. There's a smaller summer-only branch south of the city center at 4224 S Grand Blvd. Rich and poor rub elbows enjoying a 'concrete,' a delectable stirred-up combination of flavors.

St Louis Art Museum (p64)

Soulard Farmers Market   MARKET **$**
(☑ 314-622-4180; www.soulardmarket.com; 730 Carroll St; ⊙ 8am-5pm Wed & Thu, 7am-5pm Fri & Sat) A local treasure with a range of vendors selling regional produce, baked goods and prepared foods. Picnic or snack yourself silly. Dating from 1838, it's pretension-free.

Broadway Oyster Bar   CAJUN **$$**
(☑ 314-621-8811; www.broadwayoysterbar.com; 736 S Broadway; mains $10-20; ⊙ 11am-3am) Part bar, part live-music venue, but all restaurant, this joint jumps year-round. When the sun shines, people flock outside where they suck down crawfish and other Cajun treats. It's nuts before and after Cardinals games.

Shaved Duck   AMERICAN **$$**
(☑ 314-776-1407; www.theshavedduck.com; 2900 Virginia Ave; mains $10-20; ⊙ 11am-9pm Mon, to 10pm Tue-Sat) A South Grand stalwart, the Shaved Duck fires up its grills early in the day and turns out excellent barbecue, including the signature smoked duck. Options include fab sandwiches and veggie sides. Live music weeknights.

Eleven Eleven Mississippi   MODERN AMERICAN **$$**
(☑ 314-241-9999; www.1111-m.com; 1111 Mississippi Ave; mains $9-25; ⊙ 11am-10pm Mon-Thu, to midnight Fri, 5pm-midnight Sat; ☑) This popular bistro and wine bar fills an old shoe factory. Dinner mains draw on regional specialties

with a farm-to-table vibe. Other options on the seasonal menu include sandwiches, pizzas, steaks and veggie dishes. Excellent wine selection.

🍷 Drinking

Laclede's Landing, Soulard and the Loop are loaded with pubs and bars, many with live music. Most bars close at 1:30am, though some have 3am licenses.

The Grove, a strip of Manchester Ave between Kingshighway Blvd and S Vandeventer Ave, is the hub of St Louis' LGBTIQ+ community. Peruse *Vital Voice* (www.thevitalvoice.com) for info.

Blueberry Hill   BAR
(☑ 314-727-4444; www.blueberryhill.com; 6504 Delmar Blvd; ⊙ 11am-late) St Louis native Chuck Berry rocked the small basement bar here until the day he died. The venue hosts bands big and small and has good pub food (mains $8 to $15), arcade games, darts and walls covered in pop-culture artifacts.

Bridge Tap House & Wine Bar   BAR
(☑ 314-241-8141; www.thebridgestl.com; 1004 Locust St; ⊙ 11am-1am Mon-Sat, to midnight Sun) Slip onto a sofa or rest your elbows on a table at this romantic bar where you can savor fine wine or the best local beer (55 on tap) and nibble a variety of exquisite little bites from a seasonal menu.

Mud House   CAFE

(☑314-776-6599; www.themudhousestl.com; 2101 Cherokee St; ☺7am-5pm; ☎) Chemex coffees, loose-leaf teas and a great breakfast menu with many veggie options (try the Vegan Slinger!) make this funky Cherokee St staple an ideal morning stop.

☆ Entertainment

Check the *Riverfront Times* (www.riverfronttimes.com) for updates on entertainment options around town. Purchase tickets for most venues through MetroTix (www.metrotix.com).

Venice Cafe   BLUES, JAZZ

(☑314-772-5994; www.thevenicecafe.com; 1903 Pestalozzi St; ☺4pm-1am Mon-Sat) A true cabinet of curiosities. The interior of this two-level club is a master class in mosaics, while the rambling outdoor garden is chockfull of folk art and twinkling lights. Best of all, the drinks are cheap and there's live blues and jazz seven days a week.

❶ Information

Explore St Louis (☑314-421-1023; www.explorestlouis.com; cnr 7th St & Washington Ave, America's Center; ☺8am-5pm Mon-Sat; ☎) An excellent resource, with other branches in Kiener Plaza (corner of 6th and Chestnut) and at the airport.

Forest Park Visitor & Education Center (☑314-367-7275; www.forestparkforever.org; 5595 Grand Dr; ☺6am-8pm Mon-Fri, to 7pm Sat & Sun) Located in an old streetcar pavilion and has a cafe. Free walking tours leave from here, or you can take an iPod audio tour.

Missouri Welcome Center (☑314-869-7100; www.visitmo.com; Riverview Dr, I-270 exit 34; ☺8am-5pm Mon-Sat)

❶ Getting Around

Metro (www.metrostlouis.org) runs local buses and the MetroLink light-rail system (which connects the airport, the Loop, Central West End, the Gateway Transportation Center/Union Station and Downtown). Buses 30 and 40 serve Soulard from Downtown. A single/day pass is $2.50/7.50.

St Louis County Cabs (☑314-991-5300, text 314-971-8294; www.countycab.com) Call, text or book online.

OKLAHOMA

Oklahoma gets its name from the Choctaw name for 'Red People.' One look at the state's vividly red earth and you'll wonder if the name is more of a sartorial than an ethnic comment. Still, with 39 tribes located here, it is a place with deep Native American significance. Museums, cultural displays and more abound.

The other side of the Old West coin, cowboys also figure prominently in the Sooner State. Although pickups have replaced horses, there's still a great sense of the open range, interrupted only by urban Oklahoma

KANSAS

Only 13 miles of Route 66 pass through the southeast corner of Kansas, but it's a good drive along Hwy 66 and US 69 (from east to west).

Three miles down the road is Riverton; here you might consider a detour 20 miles north to Crawford County, where legendary fried chicken is a hallmark of six famous restaurants around Pittsburg. Try one of the best, Chicken Mary's (☑620-231-9510; 1133 E 600th Ave; meals from $7; ☺4-8:30pm Tue-Sat, 11am-8pm Sun).

Cross US 400 and stay on old Route 66 to the 1923 Rainbow Bridge, the last marsh arch bridge remaining on the route.

From the bridge, it's less than 3 miles south to Baxter Springs, the site of a Civil War massacre and numerous bank robberies. A restored 1939 Phillips 66 gas station is the Kansas Route 66 Visitor Center (☑620-856-2385; www.baxterspringsmuseum.org; cnr 10th St & Military Ave; ☺10am-4:30pm Tue-Sat, 1-4pm Sun). Military Ave (US 69A) takes you into Oklahoma.

City and Tulsa. Oklahoma's share of Route 66 links some of the Mother Road's iconic highlights and there are myriad atmospheric old towns.

ⓘ Information

Oklahoma Bed & Breakfast Association (www.okbba.com)

Oklahoma Tourism & Recreation Department (☑ 800-652-6552; www.travelok.com)

Oklahoma State Parks (www.travelok.com/state_parks) Most parks are free for day use; campsites cost $14 to $25 per night, and some are reservable. The website is a labyrinth.

Tulsa

Self-billed as the 'Oil Capital of the World,' Tulsa has never dirtied its hands much on the black gold that oozes out elsewhere in the state. Rather, it is home to scores of energy companies that make their living drilling for oil, selling it or supplying those who do. The steady wealth this provides helped to create Tulsa's richly detailed art-deco downtown.

Today Tulsa suffers more than most from suburban sprawl, although the Brady Arts District downtown is a bright spot.

◉ Sights

Downtown Tulsa has so much art-deco architecture it was once known as the 'Terra-Cotta City.' The Philcade Building (www.tulsaartdecomuseum.com; 511 S Boston Ave; ⊙museum 8am-6pm Mon-Fri), with its glorious T-shaped lobby, and the Boston Avenue United Methodist Church (www.bostonavenue.org; 1301 S Boston St; ⊙8:30am-5pm Mon-Fri, 8am-5pm Sun, guided tours noon Sun), rising at the end of downtown, are two exceptional examples. Download a walking guide at www.visittulsa.com by searching for 'downtown Tulsa self-guided walking tour.'

The developing Brady Arts District is centered on Brady and Main Sts immediately north of downtown. It has galleries, venues and good restaurants.

Gilcrease Museum — MUSEUM
(☑ 918-596-2700; www.gilcrease.org; 1400 Gilcrease Museum Rd; adult/child $8/free; ⊙10am-5pm Tue-Sun) Northwest of downtown, off Hwy 64, this superb museum sits on the manicured estate of a Native American who discovered oil on his allotment. Exhibits explore Native American art, textiles, pottery

Oklahoma Jazz Hall of Fame, Tulsa

and more, while the surrounding gardens make for a great stroll.

Woody Guthrie Center — MUSEUM
(☑ 918-574-2710; www.woodyguthriecenter.org; 102 E MB Brady St; adult/child $8/6; ⊙10am-6pm Tue-Sun) Woody Guthrie gained fame for his 1930s folk ballads that told stories of the Dust Bowl and the Great Depression. His life and music are recalled in this impressive museum, where you can listen to his music and explore his legacy via the works of Dylan and more. Come back on select evenings for after-hours concerts at the on-site theater (check the website for dates and times).

Oklahoma Jazz Hall of Fame — MUSEUM
(☑ 918-928-5299; www.oklahomajazz.org; 111 E 1st St; Sun jazz concerts adult/child $15/5; ⊙9am-5pm Mon-Fri, live music 6-10pm Tue & 4-7:30pm Sun) FREE Tulsa's beautiful Union Station is filled with sound again, but now it's melodious as opposed to cacophonous. During the first half of the 20th century, Tulsa was literally at the crossroads of American music with performers both homegrown and from afar. Learn about greats like Charlie Christian, Ernie Fields Senior and Wallace Willis in detailed exhibits. Sunday jazz concerts are played in the once-segregated grand concourse. On Tuesday nights there are free jam sessions.

🛏 Sleeping

Chain motels aplenty line Hwy 244 and I-44, especially at the latter's exits 229 and 232. You can also recapture some of the adventure of Route 66 at several vintage motels on E 11th St, although quality varies widely.

Desert Hills Motel
MOTEL $

(☏918-834-3311; 5220 E 11th St; r from $45; ᴾ❋ 🐾) The glowing neon cactus out front beckons you in to this lovingly restored 1950s motor court featuring 50 rooms (with refrigerators and microwaves) arranged diagonally around the parking lot. It's 5 miles east of downtown, on historic Route 66.

Hotel Campbell
HOTEL $$

(☏918-744-5500; www.thecampbellhotel.com; 2636 E 11th St; r $140-210; ᴾ❋@🐾) Restored to its 1927-era Route 66 splendor, this historic hotel east of downtown has 26 luxurious rooms with hardwood floors and plush period furniture. Ask for a tour.

Hotel Ambassador
HOTEL $$$

(☏918-587-8200; www.ambassadortulsa.com; 1324 S Main St; r $200-300; ᴾ❋@🐾) Wander along the hallway to look at the photos of this 1929 nine-story hotel before its opulent renovation. Public spaces are suitably grand; the 55 rooms are renovated and have a contemporary feel that helps the somewhat close quarters seem a tad larger.

🍴 Eating & Drinking

Look for dining options in the Brookside neighborhood, on Peoria Ave between 31st and 51st Sts; on Historic Cherry St (now 15th St) just east of Peoria Ave; and in the Brady Arts District.

Elmer's
BARBECUE $

(www.elmersbbqtulsa.com; 4130 S Peoria Ave; mains $7-17; ⊙11am-8pm Tue-Thu, to 9pm Fri & Sat) A legendary barbecue joint where the star of the menu is the potentially deadly 'Badwich,' a bun-crushing combo of superbly smoked sausages, ham, beef, pork and more. There's also smoked salmon and a showstopping side: green beans with chunks of succulent rib meat. The dining room is bright and has a house piano for the blues.

Ike's Chili House
DINER $

(☏918-838-9410; www.ikeschilius.com; 1503 E 11th St; mains $5-9; ⊙10am-7pm Mon-Fri, to 3pm Sat) Ike's has been serving chili for more than

100 years and its classic version is much-loved. You can get it straight or served over Fritos, a hot dog, fries or spaghetti. Top with red peppers, onions, jalapeños, saltines and cheddar cheese for pure joy.

Tavern
AMERICAN $$

(☏918-949-9801; www.taverntulsa.com; 201 N Main St; mains $15-38; ⊙11am-11pm Sun-Thu, to 1am Fri & Sat) This beautiful pub is a top choice in the Brady Arts District and serves excellent fare. The hamburgers here are legendary or you could opt for steaks, salads or seasonal specials. The bartenders are true mixologists and there's a good wine list.

American Solera
BREWERY

(☏918-949-4318; www.americansolera.com; 1801 S 49th W Ave; ⊙5-9pm Wed, 5-8pm Thu, 4-9pm Fri, noon-9pm Sat) Located amid the oil refineries on the outskirts of town, this tasting room is the long-awaited showpiece for American Solera's award-winning brews. Arriving feels like showing up at your old friend's garage for an impromptu party. Try the Norton Fellowship, a sour ale made with the native Norton grape.

☆ Entertainment

The *Tulsa Voice* (www.thetulsavoice.com) has the scoop of what's going on.

Cain's Ballroom
LIVE MUSIC

(☏918-584-2306; www.cainsballroom.com; 423 N Main St) Rising rockers grace the boards where Bob Wills played Western swing in the '30s and the Sex Pistols caused confusion in 1978 (check out the hole Sid Vicious punched in a wall).

Admiral Twin Drive-In
OUTDOOR CINEMA

(☏918-878-8099; www.admiraltwindrivein.com; 7355 E Easton St; adult/child $7/3; ⊙Fri-Sun evenings Mar-Sep) A classic Route 66 drive-in with two screens playing the latest Hollywood blockbusters. Make sure you arrive well before showtime to get a good spot.

Oklahoma City

Often abbreviated to OKC, Oklahoma City is nearly dead-center in the state and is the cultural and political capital. It has worked hard over the years to become more than just a cow town, all without turning its back on its cowboy heritage. It makes a good pause on your Route 66 travels.

The city is forever linked to the 1995 bombing of the Alfred P Murrah Federal Building; the memorials to this tragedy are moving.

○ Sights

Oklahoma City
National Memorial Museum · MUSEUM
(www.oklahomacitynationalmemorial.org; 620 N Harvey Ave; adult/student $15/12; ⊙9am-6pm Mon-Sat, noon-6pm Sun, last ticket sold 1hr before close) The story of America's worst incident of domestic terrorism is told at this poignant museum, which avoids becoming mawkish and lets the horrible events speak for themselves. The Outdoor Symbolic Memorial features *Field of Empty Chairs*: 168 chair sculptures for each of the people killed in the attack (the 19 small ones are for the children who perished).

National Cowboy
& Western Heritage Museum · MUSEUM
(✆405-478-2250; www.nationalcowboymuseum .org; 1700 NE 63rd St; adult/child $12.50/6; ⊙10am-5pm Mon-Sat, noon-5pm Sun) Only the smells are missing. Vibrant historic displays are complemented by a mock frontier village and an excellent collection of Western painting and sculpture featuring many works by Charles M Russell and Frederic Remington.

Stockyards City · AREA
(www.stockyardscity.org; Agnew Ave & Exchange Ave) You'll brush up against real cowboys in Stockyards City, southwest of downtown, either in the shops and restaurants that cater to them or at the Oklahoma National Stockyards, the world's largest stocker and feeder cattle market.

Oklahoma History Center · MUSEUM
(www.okhistory.org/historycenter; 800 Nazih Zuhdi Dr; adult/child $7/4; ⊙10am-5pm Mon-Sat) Near the capitol, this museum makes people the focus as it tells the story of the Sooner State through interactive exhibits.

State Capitol · LANDMARK
(✆405-521-3356; 2300 N Lincoln Blvd; ⊙7am-7pm Mon-Fri, 9am-4pm Sat & Sun, tours 9am-3pm Mon-Fri) FREE Built in 1917 (though it only got its dome in 2002), this Greco-Roman building has large murals, beautiful stained-glass windows, a tribal flag plaza and rotating art exhibits. Appropriately it's the only state capitol surrounded by working oil wells.

> ### COWBOY OUTFITS
> You can buy all forms of Western wear and gear at Langston's (✆405-235-9536; www.langstons.com; 2224 Exchange Ave; ⊙10am-8pm Mon-Sat, noon-5pm Sun). The boot selection alone is mind-blowing.

Paseo Arts District · AREA
(www.thepaseo.org; NW 30th St & Paseo) With its Spanish Revival architecture, lively bars and funky art galleries, this is OKC's most bohemian corner.

🛏 Sleeping

Many older motels line I-35 south of town; newer chain properties stack up along I-44, the NW Expwy/Hwy 3 and at Bricktown (which puts you near nightlife action).

Lincoln Inn · MOTEL $
(✆405-528-7563; www.lincolninnokc.com; 5405 N Lincoln Blvd; r from $45; P✳☎⊠☂) The best of OKC's budget options, located off I-44 not far from the State Capitol building. There's a big pool, a small gym and interior-access rooms.

JACOB CLAUSNITZER / SHUTTERSTOCK ©

Field of Empty Chairs, Oklahoma City National Memorial Museum

Oklahoma City

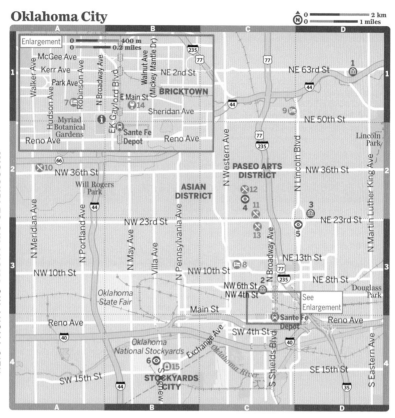

Colcord Hotel BOUTIQUE HOTEL **$$**
(☎405-601-4300; www.colcordhotel.com; 15 N
Robinson Ave; r $170-240; P❋@☎) OKC's first
skyscraper, built in 1911, is now a luxurious
12-story hotel. Many original flourishes,
such as the marble-clad lobby, survive, while
the 108 rooms have a stylish, contemporary
touch. It's near Bricktown.

Grandison Inn at Maney Park B&B **$$**
(☎405-232-8778; www.grandisoninn.com; 1200
N Shartel Ave; r $140-190; P❋☎) In a genteel
quarter of OKC just northwest of downtown,
this gracious 1904-vintage B&B features
eight rooms with period charm and modern
amenities. The house has amazing wood-
work, including a showstopping staircase.

✖ Eating

For listings, check out the weekly *Oklahoma
Gazette* (www.okgazette.com) or just head to
the renovated warehouses in the Bricktown

District, which contain a vast array of bars
and restaurants – some good, some purely
chain.

Ann's Chicken Fry House SOUTHERN US **$**
(☎405-943-8915; 4106 NW 39th St; mains $5-
12; ⊙11am-8:30pm Tue-Sat) Part real diner,
part tourist attraction, Ann's is a Route 66
veteran renowned for its – you guessed it –
chicken fried steak. Okra and cream gravy
also star, and the fried chicken lives up to
the rep. Get the black-eyed peas.

Tucker's Onion Burgers BURGERS **$**
(☎405-609-2333; www.tuckersonionburgers.com;
324 NW 23rd St; mains $5.50-10; ⊙11am-9pm) ✿
A new kind of burger joint with an old-time
Route 66 vibe, Tucker's has high-quality
food (locally sourced) that includes iconic
Oklahoma onion burgers, fresh-cut fries
and shakes. It even has a green ethos and
a fine patio.

Oklahoma City

Picasso's Cafe MODERN AMERICAN **$$**
(☑405-602-2002; www.picassosonpaseo.com;
3009 Paseo; mains $10-20; ⊗11am-late; ✎) Picasso's is renowned for its Bloody Marys
at noon and masterfully plated farm-fresh
meals. The place has an artistic sensibility,
with works by local artists on display. Grab
a table outside.

Cheever's Cafe MODERN AMERICAN **$$**
(☑405-525-7007; www.cheeverscafe.com; 2409
N Hudson ave; mains $10-40; ⊗11am-9pm Sun-
Thu, to 10:30pm Fri & Sat) This former art-
deco flower shop is now an upscale cafe with
excellent Southern- and Mexican-influenced
fare. The menu changes seasonally and is locally sourced. The ice-cream-ball dessert fills
many a dream.

Cattlemen's Steakhouse STEAK **$$**
(☑405-236-0416; www.cattlemensrestaurant.
com; 1309 S Agnew Ave; mains $7-30; ⊗6am-10pm
Sun-Thu, to midnight Fri & Sat) OKC's most sto-
ried restaurant, this Stockyards City (p69)
institution has been feeding cowpokes and
city slickers slabs of beef since 1910. Deals
are still cut at the counter (where you can
jump the wait for tables) and back in the
luxe booths.

Drinking & Nightlife

Kick up your cowboy boots and learn some
country line-dancing skills at one of OKC's
country-and-western clubs, which are scat-
tered throughout the city. For a more low-
key evening, head to the alternative-minded
Paseo Arts District (p69). To bar-hop the
night away, try Bricktown.

Bricktown Brewery BREWERY
(www.bricktownbrewery.com; 1 N Oklahoma Ave;
⊗11am-11pm Mon-Thu, to 2am Fri & Sat, to 9pm
Sun) A large microbrewery in Bricktown,
with revelers splayed out across large rooms
enjoying pool, darts and just being specta-
tors. Always hopping and has a decent food
menu.

❶ Information

Located in the Cox Convention Center, the **Okla-
homa City Visitor Information Center** (☑405-
602-5141; www.visitokc.com; 58 W Sheridan Ave;
⊗9am-6pm Mon-Fri) has tips for dining and
area attractions.

GET YOUR KICKS IN OKLAHOMA

Oklahoma's connection with America's
Main Street runs deep: the road's chief
proponent, Cyrus Avery, was a Sooner;
John Steinbeck's *Grapes of Wrath* told
of the plight of Depression-era Okie
farmers fleeing west on Route 66; and
Oklahoma has more miles of the original
alignment than any other state.

The Oklahoma Route 66 Association
(www.oklahomaroute66.com) publishes
an excellent booklet that you can pick
up from most visitor centers along the
road. It's vital because so many of the
brown-and-white Historic Route 66
signs have been stolen for souvenirs
and the original road goes by a variety
of monikers, including OK 66, US 69, US
270 etc.

Texas to Arizona

The Southwest is America's playground, luring adventurous travelers with thrilling red-rock landscapes, the legends of shoot-'em-up cowboys and the kicky delights of green chile stew.

TEXAS

Bigger than a whole heap of countries, Texas is vast, diverse and welcoming: from big-city lights to small-town simplicity, and white-sand beaches to high-country hikes.

Amarillo

Long an unavoidable stop, roughly halfway between Chicago and LA on old Route 66, Amarillo continues to figure in travel plans, simply by being the brightest light on the 543-mile stretch of I-40 between Oklahoma City, Oklahoma, and Albuquerque, New Mexico.

And though the town may seem as featureless as the surrounding landscape, there's plenty here to sate even the most attention-challenged during a road respite. Beef, the big local industry, is at the heart of Amarillo and it features in many of its attractions, including a starring role at the Big Texan Steak Ranch.

◉ Sights

American Quarter Horse Hall of Fame & Museum MUSEUM
(☑806-376-5181; www.aqha.com; 2601 I-40 E exit 72A; adult/child $6/2; ⊘9am-5pm Mon-Sat)

Quarter horses, favored on the Texas range, were originally named for their prowess at galloping down early American racetracks, which were a quarter-mile long. These beautiful animals are celebrated at this visually striking museum, which fully explores their roles in ranching and racing.

Amarillo Livestock Auction MARKET
(☑806-373-7464; www.amarillolivestockauction. com; 100 S Manhattan St; ⊘11am Mon) A slice of the real West is on display every Monday morning at the Amarillo Livestock Auction, just north of SE 3rd Ave on the city's east side. The auction is still one of the state's largest, moving more than 100,000 animals annually (from its 1970s peak of 715,000).

Wildcat Bluff Nature Center NATURE RESERVE
(☑806-352-6007; www.wildcatbluff.org; 2301 N Soncy Rd; adult/child $4/3; ⊘dawn-dusk) Stretch those road legs at this 600-acre nature center, which has trails winding through grasslands, cottonwoods and bluffs. Spy on a prairie-dog town and try to spot a burrowing owl or porcupine while avoiding rattlesnakes and tarantulas. The center is just northwest of town, off TX 335.

American Quarter Horse Hall of Fame & Museum, Amarillo

Wonderland
Amusement Park
AMUSEMENT PARK

(📞806-383-3344; www.wonderlandpark.com; 2601 Dumas Dr, off US 87 north of the centre; $17-25; ☉Apr-Aug, hours vary; ♿) If plowing along sedately for hours on the bland interstate has you ready for a little more excitement, then careening through the double loops of this park's Texas Tornado roller coaster should shake you out of your lethargy. A fun local amusement park (ignoring the hideous garden-gnome mascot), Wonderland has thrill rides, family rides and a water park. Check the online calendar for specific opening days and hours.

🛏 Sleeping

With the notable exception of the Big Texan Inn, most of Amarillo's motel accommodations are chains (in fact, there can't be one brand missing from the endless slew along I-40). Exits 64, 65 and 71 all have clusters.

Big Texan Inn
MOTEL $

(📞800-657-7177; www.bigtexan.com; 7700 I-40 E, exit 74; r $70-100; ❄🛜🖥🏊) The hotel part of Amarillo's star attraction has 54 rooms with fussy Old West details behind a faux heritage facade. The real highlight – besides the modest prices – is the outside pool in the shape of Texas. Should you try the huge steak challenge, even crawling across the parking lot to collapse in your room may be beyond you.

Best Western Santa Fe
MOTEL $$

(📞806-372-1885; www.bestwestern.com; 4600 I-40; r $80-140; 🅿❄@🛜🖥🏊) Modern motel with a large outdoor pool. Rooms are decorated with a range of grays and tans.

🍴 Eating & Drinking

At first burp, Amarillo seems awash in chain eateries along the I-40 frontage roads, but delve a little deeper to find some gems, especially along SW 6th Ave. However, don't close your eyes to everything on I-40, as Amarillo's top attraction, the Big Texan, awaits.

Most restaurants open for dinner have a bar. The Golden Light Cantina is a good place for a beer and music.

Big Texan Steak Ranch
STEAK $$

(www.bigtexan.com; 7701 I-40 E, exit 75; mains $10-40; ☉7am-10:30pm; ♿) A classic, hokey Route 66 roadside attraction, the Big Texan made the move when I-40 opened in 1971 and has never looked back. Stretch-Cadillac limos with steer-horn hood ornaments offer free shuttles to and from area motels, marquee lights blink above, a shooting arcade pings inside the saloon, and a big, tall Tex road sign welcomes you (after taunting billboards for miles in either direction).

Tyler's Barbeque
BARBECUE $

(📞806-331-2271; http://tylersbarbeque.com; 2014 Paramount Blvd; mains $8-15; ☉11am-8pm) Amarillo's favorite spot for barbecue

73

is worth the love. The line is always long, so get there early because when it sells out, it closes. The mesquite-grilled meats (the ribs and brisket are tops) are redolent with smoke. Get a seat so you can watch the west Texas sunset.

Golden Light Cantina
BURGERS **$**

(☑ 806-374-9237; www.goldenlightcafe.com; 2908 SW 6th Ave; ☺ cafe 11am-10pm, bar 4pm-2am) Classic cheeseburgers, home-cut fries, green chili stew and cold beer have sated travelers on Route 66 at this modest brick dive since 1946. On many nights there's live country and rock music in the atmospherically sweaty adjoining cantina.

Crush Wine Bar & Deli
AMERICAN **$$**

(☑ 806-418-2011; www.crushdeli.com; 701 S Polk St; mains $10-33; ☺ 11am-11pm Mon-Thu, to 12:30am Fri & Sat) Folks in suits and skirts and cowboy boots flock here for Amarillo's best beer and wine selection plus fare that goes beyond the beefy local vibe. Salads, tapas and creative light fare are ideally enjoyed outside on the patio. Crush anchors a small nightlife district downtown.

ℹ Information

Texas Travel Information Center (☑ 806-335-1441; 9700 E I-40, exit 76; ☺ 8am-5pm, to 6pm summer; ☎) An excellent resource, with vast amounts of info at a handy freeway rest stop.

For local visitor information, see the website www.visitamarillotx.com.

The Amarillo Independent (www.amarilloindy. com) is a frisky, free weekly with full local event info and an alternative viewpoint.

NEW MEXICO

They call this the Land of Enchantment for a reason. Maybe it's the drama of sunlight and shadow playing out across juniper-speckled hills, or the traditional mountain villages of horse pastures and adobe homes. Maybe it's the centuries-old towns on the northern plateaus, overlooked by the magnificent Sangre de Cristos, or the volcanoes, canyons and vast desert plains spread beneath an even vaster sky. The beauty casts a powerful spell. Mud-brick churches filled with sacred art, ancient Indian pueblos, real-life cowboys and legendary outlaws, chile-smothered enchiladas – all add to the pervasive sense of otherness that often makes New Mexico feel like a foreign country.

Maybe the state's all-but-indescribable charm is best expressed in the iconic paintings of Georgia O'Keeffe. The artist herself exclaimed, on her very first visit: 'Well! Well! Well!... This is wonderful! No one told me it was like this.'

But seriously, how could they?

Vintage Texaco gas station, Tucumcari

Tucumcari

The largest I-40 town between Albuquerque and Amarillo, Tucumcari is a ranching and farming community sited between the mesas and the plains that's also home to one of the best-preserved sections of Route 66. Not surprisingly, it still caters to travelers, with inexpensive motels, several classic pre-interstate buildings and souvenir shops.

◎ Sights & Activities

Mesalands Dinosaur Museum   MUSEUM
(☑575-461-3466;   www.mesalands.edu/community/dinosaur-museum; 222 E Laughlin St; adult/child $6.50/4; ◎10am-6pm Tue-Sat Mar-Aug, noon-5pm Tue-Sat Sep-Feb; 🚻) This engaging museum showcases all manner of prehistoric beasts, from ferocious 40ft crocodiles to battling saber-tooth cats and the T-Rex-like Torvosaurus. Dinosaur bones are cast in bronze, which not only shows fine detail but also makes them works of art. There are plenty of hands-on exhibits for kids; one ancient monster is even fitted with a saddle for photo opportunities.

Art Murals   WALKING
Buildings on and around Route 66 in downtown Tucumcari are adorned with large murals depicting local historical highlights. The life work of artists Doug and Sharon Quarles, they can be appreciated on a mural walk that makes a great way to stretch your legs and experience Tucumcari's Route 66 legacy. Grab a map from the visitor's center and get walking.

🛏 Sleeping & Eating

While the usual chain motels cluster around the I-40 exits, Tucumcari also boasts some cool old independent motels along historic Route 66.

There are a handful of diners and barbecue joints scattered throughout town, though few are open for dinner.

Blue Swallow Motel   MOTEL $
(☑575-461-9849;   www.blueswallowmotel.com; 815 E Tucumcari Blvd; r from $75; 🕸🏠) Spend the night in this beautifully restored Route 66 motel listed on the State and National Registers of Historic Places, and feel the decades melt away. The place has a great lobby, friendly owners and vintage, uniquely decorated rooms with little chairs out on the forecourt, plus a James Dean mural, and a

NEON LIGHTS

Drive the kids down Tucumcari's main street at night, when dozens of old neon signs cast a blazing glow. Relics of Tucumcari's Route 66 heyday, the bright, flashing signs were installed by business owners in the hope of luring tired travelers to stop for the night.

classic neon sign boasting '100% refrigerated air conditioning.'

Historic Route 66 Motel   MOTEL $
(☑575-461-1212; www.tucumcarimotel.com; 1620 E Route 66; r from $42; 🕸🏠🕸) When it comes to budget digs, you can't beat this renovated motel, with giant plate-glass doors and mesa views; look for the light plane outside. The 25 rooms are cheap, clean and heads and shoulders above the usual motel stay, with comfy beds and quality pillows. Small dogs are welcome here, and it even has an espresso bar.

Kix on 66   DINER $
(☑575-461-1966; www.kixon66.com; 1102 E Tucumcari Blvd; mains $5-10; ◎6am-2pm; 🏠) Very popular morning hangout serving breakfast in all shapes and sizes, from *huevos rancheros* to biscuits and gravy, plus espresso coffees, doughnuts and lunch sandwiches.

❶ Information

Visitor Center (☑575-461-1694; www.tucumcarinm.com; 404 W Route 66; ◎8:30am-5pm Mon-Fri) Useful tourist information from the chamber of commerce.

Albuquerque

Albuquerque: it's the pink hues of the Sandia Mountains at sunset, the Rio Grande's cottonwood bosque, Route 66 diners and the hometown of Walter White and Jesse Pinkman. It's a bustling desert crossroads and the largest city in the state, yet you can still hear the howls of coyotes when the sun goes down.

Often passed over by travelers on their way to Santa Fe, Albuquerque has plenty of understated appeal beneath its gritty urban facade. Good hiking and mountain-biking trails abound just outside of town, while the city's modern museums explore Pueblo culture, New Mexican art and space. Take the time to let your engine cool as you take

Albuquerque

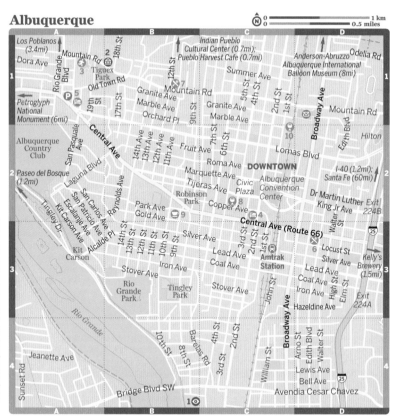

TEXAS TO ARIZONA ALBUQUERQUE

a walk among the desert petroglyphs or order up a plate of red chile enchiladas and a local beer.

Sights & Activities

Indian Pueblo Cultural Center MUSEUM
(IPCC; ☑505-843-7270; www.indianpueblo.org; 2401 12th St NW; adult/child $8.40/5.40; ⊙9am-5pm) Collectively run by New Mexico's 19 Pueblos, this cultural center makes an essential stop-off during even the shortest Albuquerque visit. The museum downstairs holds fascinating displays on the Pueblos' collective history and individual artistic traditions, while the galleries above offer changing temporary exhibitions. They're arrayed in a crescent around a plaza that's regularly used for dances and crafts demonstrations. As well as the recommended **Pueblo Harvest Cafe** (☑505-724-3510; www. indianpueblo.org; 2401 12th St NW; lunch $12-16, dinner $13-28; ⊙7am-9pm Mon-Sat, 7am-4pm

Sun; ☑⛲), there's also a large gift shop and retail gallery.

New Mexico Museum of Natural History & Science MUSEUM
(☑505-841-2800; www.nmnaturalhistory.org; 1801 Mountain Rd NW; adult/child $8/5; ⊙9am-5pm Wed-Mon; ⛲) Dinosaur-mad kids are certain to love this huge modern museum, on the northeastern fringes of Old Town. From the T Rex in the main atrium onward, it's crammed with ferocious ancient beasts. The emphasis throughout is on New Mexico, with dramatic displays on the state's geological origins and details of the impact of climate change; there's also a planetarium and large-format 3D movie theater (both of which have additional admission fees).

National Hispanic Cultural Center ARTS CENTER
(☑505-246-2261; www.nhccnm.org; 1701 4th St SW; museum adult/child $6/free; ⊙10am-5pm Tue-

Albuquerque

Sun) In the historic Barelas neighborhood, near the river a mile south of downtown, this modern, architecturally imaginative center for Hispanic visual, performing and literary arts holds three galleries used for fine arts exhibitions, performances, salsa classes and fabulous eats at Pop Fizz (p79). Check the website for upcoming events to make the most of it.

Anderson-Abruzzo Albuquerque
International Balloon Museum   MUSEUM
(☑505-768-6020;   www.balloonmuseum.com;
9201 Balloon Museum Dr;   adult/child $4/1;
⊙9am-5pm Tue-Sun) Ready to geek out on hot air balloons? This informative museum covers it all, from the first manned flight in Paris (1783) to Bernoulli's principle (how air pressure creates lift) and an actual Strato-Lab, which reached an altitude of 81,000ft in the 1950s. Take a stab at the balloon simulator here and you'll be ready for the real thing.

Petroglyph National
Monument   ARCHAEOLOGICAL SITE
(☑505-899-0205; www.nps.gov/petr; 6001 Unser Blvd NW; ⊙visitor center 8am-5pm) **FREE** The lava fields preserved in this large desert park, west of the Rio Grande, are adorned with more than 23,000 ancient petroglyphs (1000 BC to AD 1700). Several trails are scattered far

and wide: Boca Negra Canyon is the busiest and most accessible (parking $1/2 weekday/ weekend); Piedras Marcadas holds 300 petroglyphs; while Rinconada Canyon is a lovely desert walk (2.2 miles round-trip), but with fewer visible petroglyphs.

Take exit 154 off I-40 to reach the visitor center, 5.5 miles northwest of Old Town. The trails are several miles to the north and south of the center.

Paseo del Bosque   CYCLING, MOUNTAIN BIKING
(⊙dawn-dusk) A 16-mile multi-use path along the Rio Grande, the Paseo del Bosque is one of Albuquerque's gems. While the paved portion offers easy car-free riding for cyclists, what really makes it special – and beautiful – is the network of trails hidden between the pavement and river. If you rent a mountain bike, you'll have plenty of fun veering through miles of floodplains forest.

Possible stops on the Paseo del Bosque include the BioPark, the Hispanic Cultural Center (p76) – and popsicles at Pop Fizz (p79) – and the family-friendly Rio Grande Nature Center.

Sandia Peak
Mountain Biking   MOUNTAIN BIKING
(☑505-242-9052;   http://sandiapeak.com;   day pass $22, rental package $58;   ⊙10am-4pm Sat & Sun Jul & Aug) On summer weekends, the Sandia Peak ski area opens for mountain bikers, making for some long, exhilarating downhill rides. You can either rent a bike at the base facility or ride the chairlift to the

---

ALBUQUERQUE OLD TOWN

Some of the quaint adobe buildings that line the alleyways of Old Town began life as private residences in 1706, when the first 15 Spanish families called the newly named 'Alburquerque' their home (yes, it originally had an extra 'r', which somehow got lost after the Americans took over). Until the arrival of the railroad in 1880, Old Town Plaza was the hub of daily life. With many museums, galleries and original buildings within walking distance, this is the city's most popular tourist area. As you walk around, keep your mind's eye trained partly on the past. Imagine this area as it began, with a handful of hopeful families grateful to have survived a trek across hundreds of miles of desert wilderness.

top of the peak with your own bike. Unfortunately, you cannot take bikes on the tram.

🎉 Festivals & Events

International Balloon Fiesta   BALLOONING
(www.balloonfiesta.com; ⊙early Oct) This is the largest balloon festival in the world. You simply haven't lived until you've seen a three-story-tall Tony the Tiger land in your hotel courtyard, and that's exactly the sort of thing that happens during the International Balloon Fiesta, which features mass dawn take-offs on each of its nine days, overlapping the first and second weekends in October.

🛏 Sleeping

Although Albuquerque is home to about 150 hotels – all of which fill during the International Balloon Fiesta and the Gathering of Nations – few are in any way exceptional. If you're looking for character or charm, a B&B is a better option.

Andaluz   BOUTIQUE HOTEL **$$**
(✆505-242-9090; www.hotelandaluz.com; 125 2nd St NW; r from $174; P✳@🛜🐾) Albuquerque's finest historic hotel, built in the heart of downtown in 1939, has been comprehensively modernized while retaining period details like its stunning central atrium, where cozy arched nooks hold tables and couches. Rooms feature hypoallergenic bedding and carpets, the **Más Tapas Y Vino**

(✆505-923-9080; www.hotelandaluz.com; 125 2nd St NW; tapas $6-16, mains $26-36; ⊙7am-2pm & 5-9:30pm) restaurant is notable, and there's a rooftop bar. Reserve 30 days in advance for the best rates.

Böttger Mansion   B&B **$$**
(✆505-243-3639; www.bottger.com; 110 San Felipe St NW; r $115-159; P✳@🛜) The friendly proprietor gives this well-appointed B&B, built in 1912 and one minute's walk from the plaza, an edge over tough competition. Three of its seven themed, antique-furnished rooms have pressed-tin ceilings, one has a Jacuzzi tub, and sumptuous breakfasts are served in a honeysuckle-lined courtyard loved by bird-watchers. Past guests include Elvis, Janis Joplin and Machine Gun Kelly.

Los Poblanos   B&B **$$$**
(✆505-344-9297; www.lospoblanos.com; 4803 Rio Grande Blvd NW; r $230-450; P✳@🛜🏊) This amazing 20-room B&B, on a 1930s rural ranch that's a National Historic Place, is five minutes' drive north of Old Town. Close to the Rio Grande, it's set amid 25 acres of gardens, lavender fields (blooming mid-June through July) and an organic farm. The gorgeous rooms feature kiva fireplaces, while produce from the farm is served for breakfast.

BREAKING BAD IN ALBUQUERQUE

If you're a fan of the epic *Breaking Bad*, in which Walter White, a high-school chemistry teacher with lung cancer, devolves into a blue-meth kingpin named Heisenberg, you're not alone. TV viewers have been flocking to Albuquerque to follow in his blood-stained footsteps.

While the raw New Mexican landscape provided an unforgettable backdrop for the action, it's the city's real-life landmarks that have captured the most attention (in some cases too much – in 2015 creator Vince Gilligan actually had to urge fans to stop throwing pizzas on top of the White's house in a re-creation of one popular scene). You may remember the Octopus Car Wash just off Menaul Blvd at Snow Heights Circle, or fleeting glimpses of Route 66 icons such as the Dog House diner at 1216 Central Ave NW. Perhaps the most accessible of all is the excellent downtown coffee shop **Java Joe's** (p80), instantly recognizable as the gangster Tuco's mural-marked headquarters, which Heisenberg blows up during distribution negotiations.

Various *Breaking Bad* tours explore further afield, delving into the lesser-known corners of Albuquerque, where crossing some humdrum intersection may suddenly confront you with the home or workplace of a favorite character, or the scene of a memorable shootout. Our pick of the bunch is the Biking Bad cycle tour by **Routes Rentals** (✆505-933-5667; www.routesrentals.com; 404 San Felipe St NW; 4/24hr rental $25/35; ⊙8am-6pm).

Zuni performance, Albuquerque

🍴 Eating

Albuquerque offers plenty of definitive down-home New Mexican grub, plus the region's widest variety of international cuisines. Many traditional eateries are only open from 6am to 2pm (ie no dinner) – if local flavors are a priority, make sure you plan around these hours. More sophisticated dinner options lean more modern American.

Pop Fizz　　　　　　　　　　MEXICAN **$**
(📞505-508-1082; www.pop-fizz.net; 1701 4th St SW, National Hispanic Cultural Center; mains $5-7.50; ⊘11am-8pm; 🛜🚷) These all-natural *paletas* (popsicles) straight-up rock: cool off with flavors such as cucumber chile lime, mango or pineapple habanero – or perhaps you'd rather splurge on a cinnamon-churro ice-cream taco? Not to be outdone by the desserts, the kitchen also whips up all sorts of messy goodness, including carne asada fries, Sonoran dogs and Frito pies.

Golden Crown Panaderia　　　BAKERY **$**
(📞505-243-2424; www.goldencrown.biz; 1103 Mountain Rd NW; mains $7-20; ⊘7am-8pm Tue-Sat, 10am-8pm Sun) Who doesn't love a friendly neighborhood cafe-bakery? Especially one in a cozy old adobe building, with gracious staff, oven-fresh bread and pizza (with green chile or blue-corn crusts), fruity empanadas, smooth espresso coffees and cookies all round? Call ahead to reserve a loaf of quick-selling green chile bread – then eat it hot, out on the patio.

Artichoke Cafe　　　MODERN AMERICAN **$$$**
(📞505-243-0200; www.artichokecafe.com; 424 Central Ave SE; lunch mains $12-19, dinner mains $16-39; ⊘11am-2:30pm & 5-9pm Mon-Fri, 5-10pm Sat) Elegant and unpretentious, this popular bistro prepares creative gourmet cuisine with panache and is always high on foodies' lists of Albuquerque's best. It's on the eastern edge of downtown, between the bus station and I-40.

🍷 Drinking

Albuquerque's bar scene, which has long focused on downtown and Nob Hill, has been enlivened by the emergence of a new breed of brewpubs across the city.

Anodyne　　　　　　　　　　　BAR
(📞505-244-1820; 409 Central Ave NW; ⊘4pm-1:30am Mon-Sat, 7-11:30pm Sun) An excellent spot for a game of pool, Anodyne is a huge space with book-lined walls, wood ceilings, plenty of overstuffed chairs, more than 100 bottled beers and great people-watching on Central Ave.

Marble Brewery　　　　　　　BREWERY
(📞505-243-2739; www.marblebrewery.com; 111 Marble Ave NW; ⊘noon-midnight Mon-Sat, to 10:30pm Sun) A popular downtown brewpub, attached to its namesake brewery, with a

Downtown Santa Fe

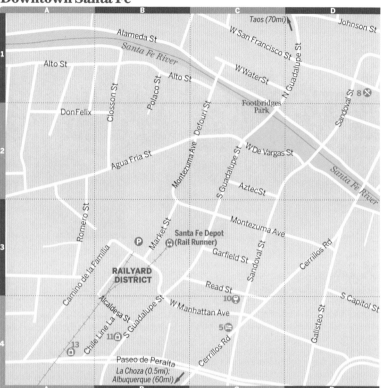

Downtown Santa Fe

snug interior for winter nights and a beer garden where bands play early-evening gigs in summer. Be sure to try its Red Ale.

Java Joe's CAFE
(✆ 505-765-1514; www.downtownjavajoes.com; 906 Park Ave SW; ◷ 6:30am-3:30pm; 🖶 😸) Best known these days for its explosive cameo role in *Breaking Bad*, this comfy coffee shop still makes a great stop-off for a java jolt or a bowl of the hottest chile in town.

Santa Fe

Welcome to 'the city different,' a place that makes its own rules without ever forgetting its long and storied past. Walking through its adobe neighborhoods, or around the busy Plaza that remains its core, there's no denying that Santa Fe has a timeless, earthy soul. Indeed, its artistic inclinations are a principal attraction – there are more quality

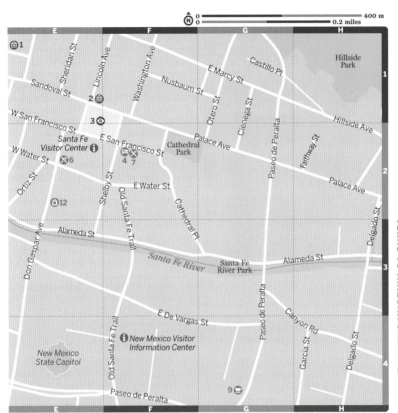

museums and galleries here then you could possibly see in just one visit.

At over 7000ft above sea level, Santa Fe is also the nation's highest state capital. Sitting at the foot of the Sangre de Cristo range, it makes a fantastic base for hiking, mountain biking, backpacking and skiing. When you come off the trails, you can indulge in chile-smothered local cuisine, buy turquoise and silver directly from Native American jewelers in the Plaza, visit remarkable churches, or simply wander along centuries-old, cottonwood-shaded lanes and daydream about one day moving here.

◉ Sights

The Plaza
PLAZA

For over 400 years, the Plaza has stood at the heart of Santa Fe. Originally it marked the far northern end of the Camino Real from Mexico; later, it was the goal for wagons heading west along the Santa Fe Trail.

Today this grassy square is peopled by tourists wandering from museum to margarita, food vendors, skateboarding kids and street musicians. Beneath the portico of the Palace of the Governors, along its northern side, Native Americans sell jewelry and pottery.

Museum of International Folk Art
MUSEUM

(☑ 505-827-6344; www.internationalfolkart.org; 706 Camino Lejo; adult/child $12/free; ⊙10am-5pm, closed Mon Nov-Apr) Santa Fe's most unusual museum centers on the world's largest collection of folk art. Its huge main gallery displays whimsical objects from more than 100 different countries. Tiny human figures go about their business in fully realized village and city scenes, while dolls, masks, toys and garments spill across the walls. Changing exhibitions in other wings explore vernacular art and culture worldwide.

Adobe architecture, Santa Fe

leries in a rambling 20th-century adobe, this museum boasts the world's largest collection of O'Keeffe's work. She's best known for her luminous New Mexican landscapes, but the changing exhibitions here range through her entire career, from her early years through her time at Ghost Ranch. Major museums worldwide own her most famous canvases, so you may not see familiar paintings, but you're sure to be bowled over by the thick brushwork and transcendent colors on show.

Museum of Indian Arts & Culture
MUSEUM
(505-476-1250; www.indianartsandculture.org; 710 Camino Lejo; adult/child $12/free; ⊙ 10am-5pm, closed Mon Sep-May) This top-quality museum sets out to trace the origins and history of the various Native American peoples of the entire Southwest, and explain and illuminate their widely differing cultural traditions. Pueblo, Navajo and Apache interviewees describe the contemporary realities each group now faces, while a truly superb collection of ceramics, modern and ancient, is complemented by stimulating temporary displays.

Georgia O'Keeffe Museum
MUSEUM
(505-946-1000; www.okeeffemuseum.org; 217 Johnson St; adult/child $12/free; ⊙ 10am-5pm Sat-Thu, to 7pm Fri) With 10 beautifully lit gal-

Meow Wolf
MUSEUM
(505-395-6369; https://meowwolf.com; 1352 Rufina Circle; adult/child $18/12; ⊙ 10am-8pm Sun, Mon, Wed, Thu, to 10pm Fri & Sat) If you've been hankering for a trip to another dimension but have yet to find a portal, the House of Eternal Return by Meow Wolf could be the place for you. The premise here is quite ingenious: visitors get to explore a re-created Victorian house for clues related to the disappearance of a California family, following a narrative that leads deeper into fragmented bits of a multiverse (often via secret passages), all of which are unique, interactive art installations.

🏃 Activities

Santa Fe's cultural attractions may be second to none, but the locals do not live on art appreciation alone. Before any strenuous activities, remember the elevation: take time to acclimatize, and watch for signs of altitude sickness. Weather changes rapidly and afternoon summer storms are frequent: always bring extra layers and a waterproof shell.

Hiking & Backpacking
Some of the best hiking and backpacking in New Mexico is right outside of Santa Fe.

CANYON ROAD GALLERY-HOPPING

Originally a Pueblo Indian footpath and later the main street through a Spanish farming community, Santa Fe's most famous art avenue embarked on its current incarnation in the 1920s, when artists led by Los Cinco Pintores (five painters who fell in love with New Mexico's landscape) moved in to take advantage of the cheap rent.

Today Canyon Rd is a top attraction, holding more than a hundred of Santa Fe's 300-plus galleries. The epicenter of the city's vibrant art scene, it offers everything from rare Native American antiquities to Santa Fe School masterpieces and in-your-face modern work. If gallery-hopping seems a bit overwhelming, don't worry, just wander.

Friday nights are particularly fun: that's when the galleries put on glittering openings, starting around 5pm. Not only are these great social events, but you can also browse while nibbling on cheese, sipping Chardonnay or sparkling cider, and chatting with the artists.

SANTA FE MARKETS

Santa Fe Indian Market (☑505-983-5220; www.swaia.org; ☺late Aug) Over a thousand artists from 100 tribes and Pueblos show work at this world-famous juried show, held the weekend after the third Thursday in August. One hundred thousand visitors converge on the Plaza, at open studios, gallery shows and the Native Cinema Showcase. Come on Friday or Saturday to see pieces competing for the top prizes; wait until Sunday before trying to bargain.

Spanish Market (www.spanishcolonial.org; ☺late Jul) Traditional Spanish Colonial arts, from *retablos* and *bultos* (carved wooden religious statues) to handcrafted furniture and metalwork, make this juried show in late July an artistic extravaganza, second only to the Indian Market.

International Folk Art Market (☑505-992-7600; www.folkartalliance.org; ☺mid-Jul) The world's largest folk art market draws around 150 artists from 50 countries to the Folk Art Museum for a festive weekend of craft shopping and cultural events in July.

The undeveloped **Pecos Wilderness**, in the heart of the **Santa Fe National Forest**, holds almost 1000 miles of trails that lead through spruce and aspen forest, across grassy alpine meadows, and up to several peaks surpassing 12,000ft. The quickest way to get above the treeline is to drive to the ski basin, hop on the **Winsor Trail** and trudge up the switchbacks. The most immediately accessible hiking trails are on the **Dale Ball Trail System** (www.santafenm. gov/trails_1), 3 miles east of downtown.

Rafting

The two rivers worth running in the vicinity of Santa Fe are the **Rio Grande** – for white-water thrills and mellow float trips – and the **Rio Chama** – mellower but better for multiday trips and arguably more scenic. Outfitters offer all sorts of variations on the basic themes, so check which options are available. Once you reserve your trip, you'll know where and what time to meet.

The rafting season generally begins in late April (depending on snowmelt), with the highest water levels in May and June. The rivers mellow out as the summer wears on, and rafting trips generally peter out by early September.

Kokopelli Rafting Adventures RAFTING
(☑505-983-3734; www.kokopelliraft.com; adult/child from $60/45; ☺mid-Apr–Aug) Runs half-day trips on the Rio Grande, and full-day trips through the Taos Box, Racecourse and the Rio Chama.

Skiing

Downhill gets most of the attention in these parts, but both the Sangre de Cris-to and Jemez mountains have numerous cross-country ski trails.

Horseback Riding

No Western fantasy is complete without hopping into a saddle. There's some great riding to be done near Santa Fe itself, as well as further afield, for example with **Broken Saddle** (☑505-424-7774; www.brokensaddle. com; off County Rd 57; rides $65-115; ⊞) in Cerrillos, and at **Ghost Ranch** (☑505-685-1000; www.ghostranch.org; US Hwy 84; day pass adult/child $5/3; ⊞) near Abiquiú.

🛏 Sleeping

When it comes to luxury accommodations, Santa Fe has a number of opulent hotels and posh B&Bs, with some unforgettable historic options within a block of the Plaza. Rates steadily diminish the further you go from downtown, with budget and national chain options strung out along Cerrillos Rd towards I-25.

Book well in advance in summer, particularly during the Indian Market and on opera nights, and also in December.

Black Canyon Campground CAMPGROUND $
(☑877-444-6777; www.recreation.gov; Hwy 475; tent & RV sites $10; ☺May–mid-Oct) A mere 8 miles from the Plaza is this gorgeous and secluded spot, complete with 36 sites and hiking and biking trails nearby. Water is available, but no hookups. If it's full, Hyde Memorial State Park is just up the road, while the Big Tesuque and Aspen Basin campgrounds (free, but no potable water) are closer to the ski area.

Chili peppers on display in a Santa Fe market

Santa Fe Motel & Inn
HOTEL $$

(📞505-982-1039; www.santafemotel.com; 510 Cerrillos Rd; r from $149, casitas from $169; P❄@🛜🐾) Close to the Railyard and a real bargain in low season, this downtown option offers motel rooms with the flavor of a Southwestern B&B, with colorful tiles, clay sunbursts and tin mirrors. The courtyard casitas cost a little more and come with kiva fireplaces and little patios. Rates include a full hot breakfast, served outdoors in summer.

La Fonda
HISTORIC HOTEL $$$

(📞800-523-5002; www.lafondasantafe.com; 100 E San Francisco St; r from $259; P❄@🛜🐾) Long renowned as the 'Inn at the end of the Santa Fe Trail,' Santa Fe's loveliest historic hotel sprawls through an old adobe just off the Plaza. Retaining its beautiful folk-art windows and murals, it's both classy and cozy, with some wonderful top-floor luxury suites, and superb sunset views from the rooftop Bell Tower Bar (100 E San Francisco St; ⊙3pm-sunset Mon-Thu, 2pm-sunset Fri-Sun May-Oct).

Eating

Food is another art form in Santa Fe, and some restaurants are as world-class as the galleries. From spicy, traditional Southwest favorites to cutting-edge cuisine, it's all here. Reservations are always recommended for the more expensive venues, especially during summer and ski season.

La Choza
NEW MEXICAN $

(📞505-982-0909; www.lachozasf.com; 905 Alarid St; lunch $8.75-12.75, dinner $10.50-18; ⊙11:30am-2pm & 5-9pm Mon-Sat; P⛓) Blue-corn burritos, a festive interior and an extensive margarita list make La Choza a perennial (and colorful) favorite among Santa Fe's discerning diners. Of the many New Mexican restaurants in Santa Fe, this one always seems to be reliably excellent. As with the Shed, its sister restaurant, arrive early or reserve.

Tia Sophia's
NEW MEXICAN $

(📞505-983-9880; www.tiasophias.com; 210 W San Francisco St; mains $7-11.75; ⊙7am-2pm Mon-Sat, 8am-1pm Sun; ✏⛓) Local artists and visiting celebrities outnumber tourists at this long-standing and always packed Santa Fe favorite. Breakfast is the meal of choice, with fantastic burritos and other Southwestern dishes, but lunch is pretty damn tasty too; try the perfectly prepared *chile rellenos* (stuffed chile peppers) or the rota of daily specials. The shelf of kids' books helps little ones pass the time.

Jambo Cafe
AFRICAN $$

(📞505-473-1269; www.jambocafe.net; 2010 Cerrillos Rd; mains $9-17; ⊙11am-9pm Mon-Sat) Hidden within a shopping center, this African-flavored cafe is hard to spot from the road; once inside, though, it's a lovely spot. It's always busy with locals who love its distinctive goat, chicken and lentil curries, veggie sandwiches and roti flatbreads, not to mention the reggae soundtrack.

El Nido
STEAK, ITALIAN $$

(☑505-954-1272; www.elnidosantafe.com; 1577 Bishops Lodge Rd; mains $11-27; ⊙4:30-9:30pm) Helmed by chef Enrique Guerrero, the culinary action at this beautiful old steakhouse revolves around the open flame, with a wood-burning grill, rotisserie and pizza oven taking center stage in the main dining room. But don't overlook the house-made pastas either (pappardelle with wild boar ragu, or Roman favorite *cacio e pepe*) – it's all simply *perfetto*. Reservations essential.

Take Bishops Lodge Rd or Hwy 285 north from Santa Fe to exit 168.

La Plazuela
NEW MEXICAN $$$

(☑505-982-5511; www.lafondasantafe.com; 100 E San Francisco St, La Fonda de Santa Fe; lunch $11-22, dinner $15-39; ⊙7am-2pm & 5-10pm Mon-Fri, 7am-3pm & 5-10pm Sat & Sun) One of Santa Fe's greatest pleasures is a meal in the Fonda's irresistible see-and-be-seen central atrium, with its excited bustle, colorful decor and high-class New Mexican food; contemporary dishes share menu space with standards like fajitas and tamales.

Cafe Pasqual's
NEW MEXICAN $$$

(☑505-983-9340; www.pasquals.com; 121 Don Gaspar Ave; breakfast & lunch $14-18.75, dinner $15-39; ⊙8am-3pm & 5:30-10pm; ✍⊡) ✎ Whatever time you visit this exuberantly colorful, utterly unpretentious place, the food, most of which has a definite south-of-the-border flavor, is worth every penny of the high prices. The breakfast menu is famous for dishes such as *huevos motuleños,* made with sautéed bananas, feta cheese and more; later on, the meat and fish mains are superb. Reservations taken for dinner only.

Drinking

Talk to 10 residents and you'll get 10 different opinions about where to find the best margarita. You may have to sample the lot to decide for yourself – get a Margarita Trail Passport ($3) at participating bars or the tourist office to help guide your way; you'll also receive a $1 discount on signature drinks.

Santa Fe Spirits
DISTILLERY

(☑505-780-5906; https://santafespirits.com; 308 Read St; ⊙3-8:30pm Mon-Thu, to 10pm Fri & Sat) The local distillery's $10 tasting flight includes an impressive amount of liquor, including shots of Colkegan single malt, Wheeler's gin and Expedition vodka. Leather chairs and exposed rafters make the in-town tasting room an intimate spot for an aperitif; fans can reserve a spot on the hourly tours of the distillery.

Kakawa Chocolate House
CAFE

(☑505-982-0388; https://kakawachocolates.com; 1050 Paseo de Peralta; ⊙10am-6pm Mon-Sat, noon-6pm Sun) Chocolate addicts simply can't miss this loving ode to the sacred bean. This isn't your mom's marshmallow-laden hot chocolate, though – these rich elixirs are based on historic recipes and divided into two categories: European (eg 17th-century France) and Meso-American (Mayan and Aztec). Bonus: it also sells sublime chocolates (prickly pear mescal) and spicy chili caramels.

Counter Culture Cafe
CAFE

(☑505-995-1105; 930 Baca St; ⊙8am-9pm Tue-Sat, to 3pm Sun & Mon; ☎) Hip hangout in the artsy Baca St compound, with loads of good food made from scratch (cinnamon rolls, lemon ricotta pancakes, tom yum soup) in addition to coffee and live music. Cash only.

Entertainment

Santa Fe Opera
OPERA

(☑505-986-5900; www.santafeopera.org; Hwy 84/285, Tesuque; backstage tours adult/child $10/ free; ⊙Jun-Aug, backstage tours 9am Mon-Fri Jun-Aug) Many visitors flock to Santa Fe for the opera alone: the theater is a marvel, with 360-degree views of sandstone wilderness crowned with sunsets and moonrises, while at center stage the world's finest talent performs masterworks. It's still the Wild West, though; you can even wear jeans. Shuttles run to and from Santa Fe ($24) and Albuquerque ($39); reserve online.

Gala festivities begin two hours before the curtain rises, when the ritual tailgate party is rendered glamorous in true Santa Fe style right in the parking lot. Bring your own caviar and brie, make reservations for the buffet dinner and lecture or a picnic dinner, or have your own caterer pour the champagne (several customize their menu to the opera's theme). **Prelude Talks**, free to all ticket holders, are offered in Stieren Orchestra Hall one and two hours before curtain.

Youth Night at the Opera offers families a chance to watch dress rehearsals for bargain rates; one precedes the run of each of the season's operas – with brief talks aimed at ages six to 22. Backstage tours offer opportunities to poke around the sets, costume and storage areas.

Shopping

Keshi
ARTS & CRAFTS

(☑505-989-8728; http://keshi.com; 227 Don Gaspar Ave; ☉10am-5pm Mon-Sat, 11am-5pm Sun) If you don't have the opportunity to visit the Zuni Pueblo, you'll at least want to visit this exquisite gallery. Specializing in Zuni fetishes (tiny animal sculptures, each with a special meaning or power), it's generally believed that the animal chooses you – not the other way around. Staff will give you plenty of time to commune with individual pieces.

Blue Rain
ART

(☑505-954-9902; www.blueraingallery.com; 544 S Guadalupe St; ☉10am-6pm Mon-Sat) This large space in the Railyard district is the top gallery in town representing contemporary Native American and regional artists. There are generally several shows on at once, encompassing everything from modern pottery and sculpture to powerful landscapes and portraits.

Santa Fe Farmers Market
MARKET

(☑505-983-4098; www.santafefarmersmarket. com; Paseo de Peralta & Guadalupe St; ☉7am-1pm Sat year-round, 7am-1pm Tue & 4-8pm Wed May-Nov; ⌖) Local produce, much of it heirloom and organic, is on sale at this spacious indoor-outdoor market, alongside homemade goodies, inexpensive food, natural body products and arts and crafts.

ⓘ Information

Santa Fe Visitor Center (☑800-777-2489; www.santafe.org; 66 E San Francisco St, Suite 3, Plaza Galeria; ☉10am-6pm) Several locations in town; most convenient is in the central Plaza Galeria.

New Mexico Visitor Information Center (☑505-827-7336; www.newmexico.org; 491 Old Santa Fe Trail; ☉8am-5pm Mon-Fri, 8am-4pm Sat & Sun) Housed in the historic 1878 Lamy Building, this friendly place offers helpful advice and free coffee.

Public Lands Information Center (☑505-954-2002; www.publiclands.org; 301 Dinosaur Trail; ☉8:30am-4pm Mon-Fri) Staff at this hugely helpful office have maps and information on public lands throughout New Mexico, and can talk you through all the hiking options.

ARIZONA

Arizona is made for road trips. Yes, the state has its showstoppers – Monument Valley, the Grand Canyon, Cathedral Rock – but you'll remember the long, romantic miles under endless skies as much as you do the icons in between. Each drive reveals a little more of the state's soul: for a dose of mom-and-pop friendliness, follow Route 66 into Flagstaff; to understand the sheer will of Arizona's mining barons, take a twisting drive through rugged Jerome; and American Indian history becomes contemporary as you drive past mesa-top Hopi villages dating back 1000 years.

Controversies about hot-button issues persistently grab headlines here. But these can't cancel out the Southwestern warmth and historical depth you'll find. And Arizo-

---

SHOPPING FOR NATIVE AMERICAN ART

Santa Fe's best shopping is beneath the *portales* (overhanging arcades) in front of the **Palace of the Governors** (☑505-476-5100; www.palaceofthegovernors.org; 105 W Palace Ave; adult/child $12/free; ☉10am-5pm, closed Mon Oct-May), to which Pueblo Indians travel as far as 200 miles to sell gorgeous handmade jewelry. The tradition started in the 1880s, when Tesuque artisans first greeted arriving trains with all manner of wares. Today up to 1200 members, representing almost every New Mexican tribe, draw lots for the 76 spaces under the vigas each morning. Those lucky enough to procure the desirable spots display bracelets, pendants, fetishes (small carved images) and thick engraved silver wedding bands on bright blankets. Classic turquoise and silver jewelry is the most popular, but you'll find many other regional stones in a rainbow of colors. Most artists are happy to tell you the story behind each piece in his or her open-air gallery – and most are one-of-a-kinds. Not only are the prices better here than in a store but the money also goes directly back to the source: the artist. Only attempt to bargain if it's suggested; the vendors may find it insulting.

Central Flagstaff

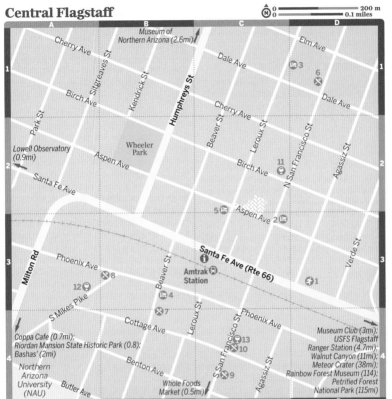

na's ancient beauty reminds you that human affairs are short-lived. The majestic Grand Canyon, the saguaro-dotted deserts of Tucson and the red rocks of Sedona...they're here for the long term.

Flagstaff

Flagstaff's laid-back charms are many, from a pedestrian-friendly historic downtown crammed with eclectic vernacular architecture and vintage neon, to hiking and skiing in the country's largest ponderosa pine forest. And the locals are a happy, athletic bunch, skewing more toward granola than gunslinger: buskers play bluegrass on street corners while cycling culture flourishes. Northern Arizona University (NAU) gives Flag its college-town flavor, while its railroad history still figures firmly in the town's identity. Throw in a healthy appreciation

Central Flagstaff

for craft beer, freshly roasted coffee beans and an all-around good time and you have the makings of the perfect northern Arizonan escape.

◉ Sights

Lowell Observatory   OBSERVATORY
(📞928-774-3358, recorded information 928-233-3211; www.lowell.edu; 1400 W Mars Hill Rd; adult/senior/child 5-17yr $15/14/8; ⊘10am-10pm Mon-Sat, to 5pm Sun; ♿) Sitting atop a hill just west of downtown Flagstaff, this national historic landmark – famous for being home to the first sighting of Pluto, in 1930 – was built by Percival Lowell in 1894. Weather permitting, visitors can still stargaze through on-site telescopes, including the famed 1896 Clark Telescope, the impetus behind the now-widely accepted theory of an expanding universe. Kids especially will love the paved Pluto Walk, which meanders through a scale model of our solar system.

Museum of Northern Arizona   MUSEUM
(📞928-774-5213; www.musnaz.org; 3101 N Fort Valley Rd; adult/senior/child 10-17yr $12/10/8; ⊘10am-5pm Mon-Sat, noon-5pm Sun; ♿) Housed inside an attractive Craftsman-style stone building beautifully situated amid a pine grove, this small but excellent museum spotlights local American Indian archaeology, history and culture, as well as geology, biology and the arts. Intriguing

Lowell Observatory
LISSANDRA MELO / SHUTTERSTOCK ©

permanent collections are augmented by temporary exhibitions on subjects such as John James Audubon's paintings of North American mammals. If you're on your way to the Grand Canyon, this museum provides a wonderful introduction to the human and natural history of the region.

Sunset Crater
Volcano National Monument   VOLCANO
(📞928-526-0502; www.nps.gov/sucr; Park Loop Rd 545; car/motorcycle/bicycle or pedestrian $20/15/10; ⊘9am-5pm Nov-May, from 8am Jun-Oct) Around AD 1064 a volcano erupted on this spot, spewing ash across 800 sq miles, spawning the Kana-A lava flow and forcing farmers to vacate lands tilled for 400 years. Now the 8029ft Sunset Crater is quiet, and mile-long trails wind through the Bonito lava flow (formed c 1180), and up Lenox Crater (7024ft). The more ambitious hikers and bikers can ascend O'Leary Peak (8965ft; 8 miles round-trip), alternatively, there is a gentle, 0.3-mile, wheelchair-accessible loop overlooking the petrified flow.

Sunset Crater is located 19 miles northeast of Flagstaff. Access fees include entry to nearby **Wupatki National Monument** (📞928-679-2365; www.nps.gov/wupa; ⊘visitor center 9am-5pm, trails sunrise-sunset; P♿), and are valid for seven days.

Walnut Canyon   RUINS
(📞928-526-3367; www.nps.gov/waca; I-40 exit 204; adult/child under 16yr $8/free; ⊘8am-5pm Jun-Oct, 9am-5pm Nov-May, trails close 1hr earlier; P) The Sinagua cliff dwellings at Walnut Canyon are set in the nearly vertical walls of a small limestone butte amid this stunning forested canyon. The mile-long **Island Trail** steeply descends 185ft (more than 200 stairs), passing 25 rooms built under the natural overhangs of the curvaceous butte. The shorter **Rim Trail** is wheelchair-accessible and affords several views of the cliff dwelling from across the canyon.

Even if you're not all that interested in the history of the Sinagua people, who abandoned the site about 700 years ago, Walnut Canyon itself is a beautiful place to visit, just 8 miles east of Flagstaff.

🏃 Activities

Scores of hiking and mountain-biking trails are easily accessed in and around Flagstaff. Fifty-six miles of trails crisscross the city as

Sunset Crater Volcano National Monument (p88)

part of the **Flagstaff Urban Trail System**; maps are available online (www.flagstaff.az.gov/futs) or you can pick one up from the Visitor Center (p95).

Stop by the USFS Flagstaff Ranger Station (p95) for information about trails in the surrounding national forest or check www.fs.fed.us. The steep three-mile hike (one-way) up 9299ft **Mt Elden** leads to a lookout at the top of the peak's tower. If it's locked when you get there, try your luck and knock: if someone happens to be there, you may be able to climb the stairs to the lookout.

Arizona Snowbowl offers several trails, including the strenuous 4.5-mile one-way hike up 12,633ft **Humphreys Peak**, the highest point in Arizona; wear decent boots as some sections of the trail cross over crumbly volcanic rock. During summer you can ride the **chairlift** (☑928-779-1951; www.arizonasnowbowl.com; 9300 N Snowbowl Rd; adult $19, senior & child 8-12yr $13; ⊙10am-4pm Fri-Sun late May–mid-Oct; ⊕) to 11,500ft, where you can hike, attend ranger talks and take in the stunning desert and mountain views. Children under eight ride for free.

Hikes abound in Grand Canyon National Park (p90), which is about 82 miles from Flagstaff.

For the inside track on the mountain-biking scene, visit the super-friendly gearheads at **Absolute Bikes** (☑928-779-5969; www.absolutebikes.net; 202 E Rte 66; bike rentals per day from $39; ⊙9am-7pm Mon-Fri, 9am-6pm Sat, 10am-4pm Sun Apr-Thanksgiving, shorter hours Dec-Mar).

🛏 Sleeping

Free dispersed camping is permitted in the Coconino National Forest surrounding Flagstaff. There are also campgrounds in Oak Creek Canyon to the south of town and Sunset Crater to the north.

Motel Dubeau HOSTEL $
(☑928-774-6731; www.modubeau.com; 19 W Phoenix Ave; dm/r from $27/53; ⓟ❄@🛜) Built in 1929 as Flagstaff's first motel, this independent hostel offers the same friendly service and clean, well-run accommodations as its sister property, Grand Canyon International Hostel. The private rooms are similar to basic, but handsome, hotel rooms, and come with refrigerators, cable TV and private bathrooms. On-site Nomads serves beer, wine and light snacks. There are also kitchen and laundry facilities.

(continued on p93)

GRAND CANYON NATIONAL PARK

No matter how much you read about the Grand Canyon or how many photographs you've seen, nothing really prepares you for the sight of it. One of the world's seven natural wonders, it's so startlingly familiar and iconic you can't take your eyes off it. The canyon's immensity, the sheer intensity of light and shadow at sunrise or sunset, even its very age, scream for superlatives.

At about two billion years old – half of earth's total life span – the layer of Vishnu Schist at the bottom of the canyon is some of the oldest exposed rock on the planet. And the means by which it was exposed is of course the living, mighty Colorado River, which continues to carve its way 277 miles through the canyon as it has for the past six million years.

While the park isn't technically on Route 66, it's close enough to make a detour.

Viewpoints

Marble Viewpoint A favorite of the many Kaibab National Forest overlooks, this viewpoint makes a spectacular picnic or camping spot. From the 1-acre meadow, covered with Indian paintbrush and hiding Coconino sandstone fossils, views extend over the eastern edge of the canyon to the paper-flat expanse beyond. This is not a quintessential Grand Canyon overlook that you'll see in postcards or Grand Canyon books. Instead, you're looking down to where the Colorado first cuts into the rocks from Lees Ferry.

The road seems to end at an overlook; be sure to take the narrow road through the woods to the right about 0.25 miles to Marble Viewpoint.

Bright Angel Point (www.nps.gov; North Rim) Short, easy and spectacular (it's just a 0.5 mile round-trip), the paved trail to Bright Angel Point is a Grand Canyon must. Beginning from the back porch of the Grand Canyon Lodge, it goes to a narrow finger of an overlook with fabulous views.

Desert View Watchtower (www.nps.gov/grca; Desert View, East Enrance; ☺ 8am-sunset mid-May–Aug, 9am-6pm Sep–mid-Oct, 9am-5pm mid-Oct–Feb, 8am-6pm Mar–mid-May) The worn winding staircase of Mary Colter's 70ft stone tower, built in 1932, leads to the highest spot on the rim (7522ft). From here, unparalleled views take in not only the canyon and the Colorado River, but also the San Francisco Peaks, the Navajo Reservation and the Painted Desert. Hopi artist Fred Kabotie's murals depicting the snake legend, a Hopi wedding and other scenes grace the interior walls, and there's a small gift shop on the 1st floor.

Shoshone Point (www.nps.gov/grca; Desert View Dr) Walk 1 mile along the mostly level dirt road to marvelously uncrowded Shoshone Point, a rocky promontory with some of the canyon's best views. This viewpoint is unmarked; look for the small parking lot about 1.2 miles east of Yaki Point.

Hikes

North Kaibab Trail (North Rim) The North Kaibab Trail is the North Rim's only maintained rim-to-river trail and connects with trails to the South Rim. The first 4.7 miles are the steepest, dropping 3050ft to Roaring Springs – a popular all-day hike.

If you prefer a shorter day hike below the rim, walk just 0.75 miles down to Coconino Overlook or two miles to the Supai Tunnel to get a taste of steep inner-canyon hiking. The 28-mile round-trip to the Colorado River is a multiday affair.

Cape Final Trail To join this easy 4-mile round-trip, which offers incredible views of the canyon, find the trailhead in an unpaved car park on the east side of the Cape Royal Rd, about 2½ miles north of the Cape Royal car park.

Bright Angel Trail The most popular of the corridor trails is the beautiful Bright Angel Trail. The steep and scenic 7.8-mile descent to the Colorado River is punctuated with four logical turnaround spots. The trailhead is just west of **Bright Angel Lodge** (www.nps.gov/grca; Village Loop Dr; ☐ Village).

Summer heat can be crippling; day hikers should either turn around at one of the two rest houses (a 3- to 6-mile round-trip) or hit the trail at dawn to safely make the longer hikes to Indian Garden and Plateau Point (9.2- and 12.2-mile round-trips respectively). Do not hike to the river in one day.

Rim Trail (www.nps.gov/grca; 🚻; 🚌 Hermits Rest, Village, Kaibab/Rim) Beginning in Grand Canyon Village, the popular Rim Trail follows the rim west 13 miles to Hermits Rest, dipping in and out of scrubby pines and connecting a series of scenic points and historical sights. Portions are paved, and every viewpoint is accessed by one of the three shuttle routes.

The western-most 2.8 mile **Greenway Trail** (www.nps.gov/grca) stretch from Monument Creek Vista to Hermits Rest accommodates bicycles and visitors in wheelchairs, and the **Trail of Time** (www.nps.gov/grca; Grand Canyon Village; 🚻; 🚌 Village) borders the Rim Trail just west of Yavapai Geology Museum. Here, every meter of the trail represents one million years of geologic history, with exhibits providing the details.

South Kaibab Trail (Yaki Point Rd, off Desert View Dr; 🚌 Kaibab/Rim) The South Kaibab is one of the park's prettiest trails, combining stunning scenery and unobstructed 360-degree views with every step. Steep, rough and wholly exposed, ascents during summer can be dangerous, and during this season rangers discourage all but the shortest day hikes – otherwise it's a grueling 7-mile round-trip to the Colorado River.

Tours

Canyon Trail Rides (☏ 435-679-8665; www.canyonrides.com; North Rim; 1hr/half-day mule ride $45/90; ⏰ schedules vary mid-May–mid-Oct) You can make reservations anytime for the upcoming year but, unlike mule trips on the South Rim, you can usually book a trip upon your arrival at the park; just duck inside the Grand Canyon Lodge to the Mule Desk. Rides don't reach the Colorado River, but the half-day trip gives a taste of life below the rim.

Rim View Walk (www.nps.gov/grca; Grand Canyon Village; ⏰ 8:30am Mon, Wed & Fri Jun-Aug) This two-hour ranger-led walk along a paved two-mile section of the Rim Trail examines natural history and contemporary Grand Canyon issues.

Food

While the South Rim has a full-sized grocery store, the North Rim General Store offers only a small but thorough selection of groceries, including diapers, alcohol and firewood. The closest full grocery store is in Kanab, a 1½-hour drive north.

Accommodations

Accommodations in the park range from historic lodges to rustic cabins and standard motel rooms. Reservations are accepted 13 months in advance. Be sure to book early, particularly if you are traveling from May through August or if you have a specific lodging in mind (for example, Phantom Ranch or a rim-side cabin on the North Rim).

All but two park lodges are on the South Rim. The North Rim offers one lodge and one campground. Below the rim, there are three maintained corridor campgrounds and several backcountry campsites, but the only lodge is Phantom Ranch.

If you're looking for a room with character, your best bets are Sedona and Flagstaff. Tusayan, the closest town to the park, caters to canyon tourists but offers little more than a short strip of tired chain motels and uninspired eateries.

Tourist Information

North Rim Visitor Center (☏ 928-638-7888; www.nps.gov/grca; ⏰ 8am-6pm May 15-Oct 15) Beside Grand Canyon Lodge, this is the place to get information on the park, and the starting point for ranger-led nature walks.

Getting There & Away

Grand Canyon National Park is about 82 miles from Flagstaff via I-40 and Hwy 64.

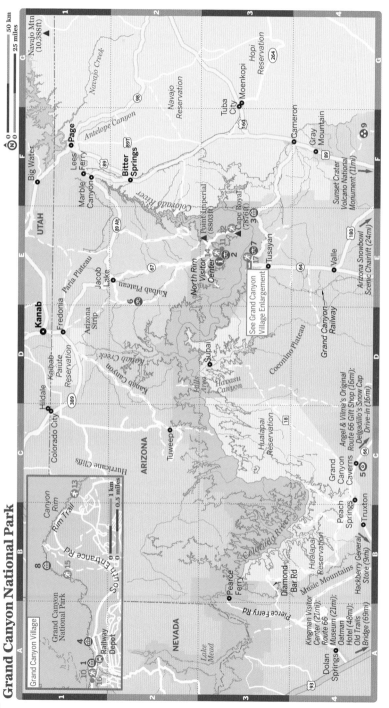

Grand Canyon National Park

Grand Canyon Village

50 km
25 miles

Navajo Mtn (10,388ft)

Navajo Creek

Page

Antelope Canyon

Big Water

Lees Ferry

Marble Canyon

Bitter Springs

Moenkopi

Hopi Reservation

Tuba City

Navajo Reservation

Cameron

Gray Mountain

Sunset Crater Volcano National Monument (11mi)

Arizona Snowbowl Scenic Chairlift (24mi)

Colorado River

UTAH

Kanab

Fredonia

Jacob Lake

Kaibab Plateau

Pania Plateau

Kaibab–Paiute Reservation

Hildale

Colorado City

Kanab Creek

Arizona Strip

North Rim Visitor Center

Point Imperial (8803ft)

Cape Royal (7876ft)

Tusayan

Valle

See Grand Canyon Village Enlargement

Grand Canyon Railway

Coconino Plateau

Supai

Havasu Canyon

Hualapai Reservation

Angel & Vilma's Original Route 66 Gift Shop (16mi); Delgadillo's Snow Cap Drive-In (16mi)

Grand Canyon Caverns

Peach Springs

Truxton

Hualapai Reservation

Hackberry General Store (9mi)

Music Mountains

Diamond Bar Rd

Colorado River

Kingman Visitor Center (21mi); Route 66 Museum (21mi); Oatman Hotel (48mi); Old Trails Bridge (69mi)

Dolan Springs

Pearce Ferry

Pierce Ferry Rd

Lake Mead

NEVADA

ARIZONA

Tuweep

Hurricane Cliffs

Canyon Rim

Rim Trail

South Entrance Rd

Grand Canyon National Park

Railway Depot

1 km
0.5 miles

Grand Canyon National Park

(continued from p89)

Inn at 410 B&B $$
(☑ 928-774-0088; www.inn410.com; 410 N Leroux St; r from $185; P ❋ 🛜) This fully renovated 1894 bed-and-breakfast offers 10 spacious, beautifully decorated and themed bedrooms, each featuring a fridge and bathroom, and many with four-poster beds and delightful views. Just a short stroll from downtown, the inn has a shady orchard-garden and a cozy dining room, where a full gourmet breakfast and afternoon snacks are served.

Hotel Monte Vista HISTORIC HOTEL $$
(☑ 928-779-6971; www.hotelmontevista.com; 100 N San Francisco St; r/ste from $115/145; ❋ 🛜) A huge, old-fashioned neon sign towers over this 1926 landmark hotel, hinting at what's inside: feather lampshades, vintage furniture, bold colors and eclectic decor. Rooms are named for the movie stars who stayed here, including the 'Humphrey Bogart,' with dramatic black walls, yellow ceiling and gold-satin bedding. Several resident ghosts supposedly make regular appearances.

🍴 Eating

Flagstaff's college population and general dedication to living well translate into one of the best dining scenes in the state. Self-caterers can try **Bashas'** (☑ 928-774-3882; www.bashas.com; 2700 S Woodlands Village Blvd; ⊙ 6am-11pm), a good local chain supermarket with a respectable selection of organic foods. For health food, there's **Whole Foods Market** (☑ 928-774-5747; www.wholefoodsmarket.com; 320 S Cambridge Lane; ⊙ 7am-9pm; 🅿).

Macy's CAFE $
(☑ 928-774-2243; www.macyscoffee.net; 14 S Beaver St; breakfast/lunch $6/7; ⊙ 6am-6pm; 🛜🅿) The delicious coffee served up at this Flagstaff institution – house roasted in the original, handsome, fire-engine-red roaster in the corner – has kept local students and caffeine devotees buzzing since the 1980s. The vegetarian menu includes many vegan choices, along with traditional cafe grub favorites such as pastries, steamed eggs, waffles, yogurt and granola, salads and veggie sandwiches.

Pizzicletta PIZZA $
(☑ 928-774-3242; www.pizzicletta.com; 203 W Phoenix Ave; pizzas $11-15; ⊙ 5-9pm Sun-Thu, to 10pm Fri & Sat) Tiny Pizzicletta, where the excellent thin-crusted wood-fired pizzas are loaded with gourmet toppings like arugula and aged prosciutto, is housed in a sliver of a white-brick building. Inside there's an open kitchen, one long table with iron chairs, Edison bulbs and industrial surrounds. You can order in while you enjoy some suds at

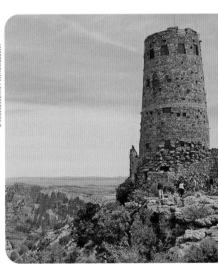

Desert View Watchtower (p90),
Grand Canyon National Park

JIM COTTINGHAM / SHUTTERSTOCK ©

TEXAS TO ARIZONA FLAGSTAFF

ROMAN KHOMLYAK / SHUTTERSTOCK ©

North Rim, as seen from the Bright Angel Trail (p90), Grand Canyon National Park

Mother Road Brewing Company (📞928-774-9139; www.motherroadbeer.com; 7 S Mikes Pike; ⏲2-9pm Mon-Thu, 2-10pm Fri, noon-10pm Sat, noon-9pm Sun) next door.

Proper Meats + Provisions DELI $
(📞928-774-9001; www.propermeats.com; 110 S San Francisco St; sandwiches $12-13; ⏲10am-7pm) Come here for house-made salami and pancetta, local grass-fed beef for the barbecue and other meat-lover delights. There's also wine, as well as an eclectic selection of non-alcoholic drinks, cheese and fresh-baked rustic bread. And don't miss the sensational sandwiches – perhaps the perenially popular seven-day pastrami with Aleppo pepper and cactus cream cheese, or the Vietnamese *banh mi* with confit pork shoulder.

Tourist Home Urban Market CAFE $
(📞928-779-2811; www.touristhomeurbanmarket.com; 52 S San Francisco St; mains $10-12; ⏲6am-8pm; 👪) Housed in a beautifully renovated 1926 house that was originally home to Basque sheepherder immigrants, this upscale market cafe serves up the best breakfast in a town full of excellent morning vittles. Try the Hash Bowl: eggs any style served on breakfast potatoes and accompanied by chorizo, spiced beets and a cilantro pesto.

Brix Restaurant & Wine Bar INTERNATIONAL $$$
(📞928-213-1021; www.brixflagstaff.com; 413 N San Francisco St; mains $30-32; ⏲5-9pm Sun & Tue-Thu, to 10pm Fri & Sat; 🖋) Brix offers seasonal, locally sourced and generally top-notch fare in a handsome room with exposed brick walls and an intimate copper bar. Sister business Proper Meats + Provisions on S San Francisco supplies charcuterie, free-range pork and other fundamentals of lip-smacking dishes that include cavatelli with Calabrese sausage, kale and preserved lemon. The wine list is well curated, and reservations are recommended.

Drinking & Nightlife

For details about festivals and music programs, call the Visitor Center (p95) or check www.flagstaff365.com. On Friday and Saturday nights in summer, people gather on blankets for free music and family movies at Heritage Sq. The fun starts at 5pm.

Pick up the free *Flagstaff Live!*, published on Thursdays, or check out www.flaglive.com for current shows and happenings around town.

Museum Club BAR
(📞928-526-9434; www.themuseumclub.com; 3404 E Rte 66; ⏲11am-2am) This honky-tonk roadhouse on Route 66 has been kicking up its heels since 1936. Inside what looks like a huge log cabin you'll find a large wooden

dance floor, animal mounts and a sumptuous elixir-filled mahogany bar. The origins of the name? In 1931 it housed a taxidermy museum.

Tinderbox Kitchen & Annex   COCKTAIL BAR
(☑ 928-226-8440;   www.tinderboxkitchen.com;
34 S San Francisco St; ⊙ 4-11pm Sun-Thu, 3pm-midnight Fri & Sat) This slinky cocktail bar mixes up great originals and classics: the Moscow Mule with mint and cucumber might just be the best cocktail in Flagstaff. The outdoor patio, actually a handball court built by Basque immigrants in 1926, attracts a low-key local crowd. Annexed to the wonderful Tinderbox Kitchen (open 5pm to 10pm) it also does poutine and other top-notch drinking food.

Hops on Birch   PUB
(☑ 928-774-4011; www.hopsonbirch.com; 22 E Birch Ave; ⊙ 1:30pm-12:30am Mon-Thu, to 2am Fri, noon-2am Sat, noon-12:30am Sun) Simple and handsome, Hops on Birch has 34 rotating beers on tap, live music five nights a week and a friendly local-crowd vibe. In classic Flagstaff style, dogs are as welcome as humans.

FLAGSTAFF CRAFT BEER

Craft-beer fans can follow the Flagstaff-Grand Canyon Ale Trail (www.flagstaffaletrail.com) to sample microbrews at downtown breweries and a bar or two. Buy a trail passport at the Visitor Center or one of the breweries listed on the website.

---

❶ Information

USFS Flagstaff Ranger Station (☑ 928-526-0866; www.fs.usda.gov; 5075 N Hwy 89; ⊙ 8am-4pm Mon-Fri) Provides information on the Mt Elden, Humphreys Peak and O'Leary Peak areas north of Flagstaff.

Visitor Center (☑ 800-842-7293, 928-213-2951; www.flagstaffarizona.org; 1 E Rte 66; ⊙ 8am-5pm Mon-Sat, 9am-5pm Sun) Located inside the Amtrak station, the visitor center has a great Flagstaff Discovery map and tons of information on things to do.

Flagstaff Medical Center (☑ 928-779-3366; https://nahealth.com; 1200 N Beaver St; ⊙ emergency 24hr) One of the nearest hospitals to the Grand Canyon South Rim.

Iconic beaches, snowcapped crags, sculpted deserts: in case you hadn't noticed, Mother Nature plays favorites with California.

California

LOS ANGELES

Ruggedly good looking, deeply creative and-with a sunny disposition to boot...if LA were on Tinder, the app would crash.

◉ Sights

◉ Hollywood

No other corner of LA is steeped in as much mythology as Hollywood. It's here that you'll find the Hollywood Walk of Fame, the Capitol Records Tower and Grauman's Chinese Theatre, where the hand- and footprints of entertainment deities are immortalized in concrete. Look beyond the tourist-swamped landmarks of Hollywood Blvd and you'll discover a nuanced, multifaceted neighborhood where industrial streets are punctuated by edgy galleries and boutiques, where strip malls hide swinging French bistros and where steep, sleepy streets harbor the homes of long-gone silver-screen stars.

Hollywood Walk of Fame   LANDMARK
(Map p98; www.walkoffame.com; Hollywood Blvd; Ⓜ Red Line to Hollywood/Highland) Big Bird, Bob Hope, Marilyn Monroe and Aretha Franklin are among the stars being sought out, worshipped, photographed and stepped on along the Hollywood Walk of Fame. Since 1960 more than 2600 performers – from legends to bit-part players – have been honored with a pink-marble sidewalk star.

Hollywood Museum   MUSEUM
(Map p98; ☑323-464-7776; www.thehollywood museum.com; 1660 N Highland Ave; adult/child $15/5; ◌10am-5pm Wed-Sun; Ⓜ Red Line to Hollywood/Highland) For a taste of Old Hollywood, do not miss this musty temple to the stars, its four floors crammed with movie and TV costumes and props. The museum is housed inside the Max Factor Building, built in 1914 and relaunched as a glamorous beauty salon in 1935. At the helm was Polish-Jewish businessman Max Factor, Hollywood's leading authority on cosmetics. And it was right here that he worked his magic on Hollywood's most famous screen queens.

Grauman's Chinese Theatre   LANDMARK
(TCL Chinese Theatres; Map p98; ☑323-461-3331; www.tclchinesetheatres.com; 6925 Hollywood Blvd; guided tour adult/senior/child $16/13.50/8; ♿; Ⓜ Red Line to Hollywood/Highland) Ever wondered what it's like to be in George Clooney's shoes? Just find his footprints in the forecourt of this world-famous movie palace. The exotic pagoda theater – complete with

Grauman's Chinese Theatre, Los Angeles

temple bells and stone heaven dogs from China – has shown movies since 1927 when Cecil B DeMille's *The King of Kings* first flickered across the screen.

◉ Los Feliz & Griffith Park

Easy-living Los Feliz – (mis)pronounced *Fee*-liz – is home to screenwriters, low-key celebrities and some legendary bars. It's here that you'll find Jeff Goldblum tickling the ivories at the Rockwell, and Marty and Elayne jazzing it up at the Dresden lounge. Walt Disney opened his first studio on Hyperion Ave and the neighborhood's lush hillside mansions have housed greats the likes of Cecil B DeMille and Norma Talmadge. North of Los Feliz lie the deep canyons and hiking trails of Griffith Park, whose own fabled icons include the mighty Griffith Observatory.

Griffith Observatory   MUSEUM
(☑ 213-473-0890; www.griffithobservatory.org; 2800 E Observatory Rd; admission free, planetarium shows adult/child $7/3; ⊙ noon-10pm Tue-Fri, from 10am Sat & Sun; P ♿; 🚍 DASH Observatory) **FREE** LA's landmark 1935 observatory opens a window onto the universe from its perch on the southern slopes of Mt Hollywood. Its planetarium claims the world's most advanced star projector, while its astronomical touch displays explore some mind-bending topics, from the evolution of the telescope and the ultraviolet x-rays used to map our solar system to the cosmos itself. Then, of course, there are the views, which (on clear days) take in the entire LA basin, surrounding mountains and Pacific Ocean.

Hollywood Sign   LANDMARK
LA's most famous landmark first appeared in the hills in 1923 as an advertising gimmick for a real-estate development called 'Hollywoodland'. Each letter is 50ft tall and made of sheet metal. Once aglow with 4000 light bulbs, the sign even had its own caretaker who lived behind the 'L' until 1939.

Autry Museum of the American West   MUSEUM
(☑ 323-667-2000; www.autrynationalcenter.org; 4700 Western Heritage Way, Griffith Park; adult/senior & student/child $14/10/6, 2nd Tue each month free; ⊙ 10am-4pm Tue-Fri, to 5pm Sat & Sun; P ♿) Established by singing cowboy Gene Autry, this expansive, underrated museum offers contemporary perspectives on the history and people of the American West, as well as their links to the region's contemporary culture. Permanent exhibitions explore everything from Native American traditions to the cattle drives of the 19th century and daily frontier life; look for the beautifully carved vintage saloon bar. You'll also find costumes and artifacts from famous Hollywood westerns such as *Annie Get Your Gun,* as well as rotating art exhibitions.

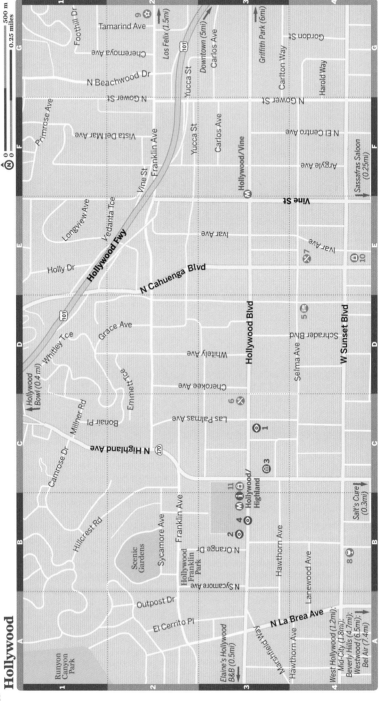

CALIFORNIA LOS ANGELES

Hollywood

98

Runyon Canyon Park

Foothill Dr

Tamarind Ave

Cheremoya Ave

Los Felix (1.5mi)

Downtown (5mi)

Carlos Ave

Griffith Park (6mi)

N Beachwood Dr

Yucca St

Carlton Way

Gordon St

Primrose Ave

N Gower St

N Gower St

Harold Way

Franklin Ave

Vista Del Mar Ave

Yucca St

Carlos Ave

N El Centro Ave

Sassafras Saloon (0.25mi)

Vine St

Hollywood/Vine

Argyle Ave

Longview Ave

Vedanta Tce

Hollywood Fwy

Vine St

Ivar Ave

Vine St

Holly Dr

N Cahuenga Blvd

Ivar Ave

Hollywood (0.4mi)

Whitley Tce

Grace Ave

Hollywood Blvd

Schrader Blvd

Selma Ave

W Sunset Blvd

Camrose Dr

Millner Rd

Bonair Pl

Emmett Tce

Whitley Ave

Cherokee Ave

Las Palmas Ave

Hillcrest Rd

Scenic Gardens

Sycamore Ave

N Highland Ave

Hollywood/Highland

Franklin Ave

Hollywood Franklin Park

N Orange Dr

Hawthorn Ave

Lanewood Ave

Salt's Cure (0.3mi)

N Sycamore Ave

Sycamore Ave

Outpost Dr

El Cerrito Pl

Elaine's Hollywood B&B (0.5mi)

Marshfield Way

Hawthorn Ave

N La Brea Ave

West Hollywood (1.2mi); Mid-City (1.8mi); Beverly Hills (4.7mi); Westwood (6.5mi); Bel Air (7.4mi)

500 m
0.25 miles

Hollywood

Griffith Park   PARK

(☑323-644-2050; www.laparks.org; 4730 Crystal Springs Dr; ◷5am-10pm, trails sunrise-sunset; ᴘᴍ) 𝐅𝐑𝐄𝐄 A gift to the city in 1896 by mining mogul Griffith J Griffith, and five times the size of New York's Central Park, Griffith Park is one of the country's largest urban green spaces. It contains (among other things) a major outdoor theater, the city zoo, an observatory, two museums, golf courses, playgrounds, 53 miles of hiking trails, Batman's caves and the famous Hollywood sign.

◉ Beverly Hills, Bel Air, Brentwood & Westwood

The major cultural sight here is the Getty Center, located in the hills of Brentwood. Westwood is home to the well-tended UCLA campus, the contemporary-art-focused Hammer Museum and the star-studded Westwood Village Memorial Park Cemetery, all three of which are within walking distance of each other. Beverly Hills claims Rodeo Dr, a prime people-watching spot. Guided tours of celebrity homes depart from Hollywood.

Rodeo Drive   STREET

It might be pricey and unapologetically pretentious, but no trip to LA would be complete without a saunter along Rodeo Dr, the famous three-block ribbon of style where sample-size fembots browse for Gucci and Dior. Fashion retailer Fred Hayman opened the strip's first luxury boutique – Giorgio Beverly Hills – at number 273 back in 1961. Famed for its striped white-and-yellow awning, the store allowed its well-heeled clients to sip cocktails while shopping and have their purchases home delivered in a Rolls-Royce.

Getty Center   MUSEUM

(☑310-440-7300; www.getty.edu; 1200 Getty Center Dr, off I-405 Fwy; ◷10am-5:30pm Tue-Fri & Sun, to 9pm Sat; ᴘᴍ; ᵔ734, 234) 𝐅𝐑𝐄𝐄 In its billion-dollar, in-the-clouds perch, high above the city grit and grime, the Getty Center presents triple delights: a stellar art collection (everything from medieval triptychs to baroque sculpture and impressionist brushstrokes), Richard Meier's cutting-edge architecture, and the visual splendor of seasonally changing gardens. Admission is free, but parking is $15 ($10 after 3pm).

Museum of Tolerance   MUSEUM

(☑reservations 310-772-2505; www.museumoftolerance.com; 9786 W Pico Blvd; adult/senior/student $15.50/12.50/11.50, Anne Frank Exhibit adult/senior/student $15.50/13.50/12.50; ◷10am-5pm Sun-Wed & Fri, to 9:30pm Thu, to 3:30pm Fri Nov-Mar; ᴘ) Run by the Simon Wiesenthal Center, this powerful, deeply moving museum uses interactive technology to engage visitors in discussion and contemplation around racism and bigotry. Particular focus is given to the Holocaust, with a major basement exhibition that examines the social, political and economic conditions that led to the Holocaust, as well as the experience of the millions persecuted. On the museum's 2nd floor, another major exhibition offers an intimate look into the life and effect of Anne Frank.

◉ West Hollywood & Mid-City

Top of the list for any visit to LA is Museum Row, as Wilshire Blvd is known between about Fairfax and La Brea Aves. If nothing else, be sure to take in at least a portion of the huge Los Angeles County Museum of Art and the refurbished, very striking Petersen Automotive Museum.

CALIFORNIA LOS ANGELES

ANDREW KENNELLY / GETTY IMAGES ©

Griffith Observatory (p97)

Los Angeles County Museum of Art   MUSEUM

(LACMA; ☑323-857-6000; www.lacma.org; 5905 Wilshire Blvd, Mid-City; adult/child $15/free, 2nd Tue each month free; ⊙11am-5pm Mon, Tue & Thu, to 8pm Fri, 10am-7pm Sat & Sun; P; Ⓜ Metro lines 20, 217, 720, 780 to Wilshire & Fairfax) The depth and wealth of the collection at the largest museum in the western US is stunning. LACMA holds all the major players – Rembrandt, Cézanne, Magritte, Mary Cassat, Ansel Adams – plus millennia worth of Chinese, Japanese, pre-Columbian and ancient Greek, Roman and Egyptian sculpture. Recent acquisitions include massive outdoor installations such as Chris Burden's *Urban Light* (a surreal selfie backdrop of hundreds of vintage LA streetlamps) and Michael Heizer's *Levitated Mass,* a surprisingly inspirational 340-ton boulder perched over a walkway.

Original Farmers Market   MARKET

(☑323-933-9211; www.farmersmarketla.com; 6333 W 3rd St, Fairfax District; ⊙9am-9pm Mon-Fri, to 8pm Sat, 10am-7pm Sun; P ⊕) Long before the city was flooded with farmers markets, there was *the* farmers market. Fresh produce, roasted nuts, doughnuts, cheeses, blini – you'll find them all at this 1934 landmark. Casual and kid friendly, it's a fun place for a browse, snack or some people-watching.

Petersen Automotive Museum   MUSEUM

(☑323-930-2277; www.petersen.org; 6060 Wilshire Blvd, Mid-City; adult/senior & student/child $15/12/7; ⊙10am-6pm; P ⊕; Ⓜ Metro lines 20, 217, 720, 780 to Wilshire & Fairfax) A four-story ode to the auto, the Petersen Automotive Museum is a treat even for those who can't tell a piston from a carburetor. A headlights-to-brake-lights futuristic makeover (by Kohn Pederson Fox) in late 2015 left it fairly gleaming from the outside; the exterior is undulating bands of stainless steel on a hot-rod-red background. The once-dowdy inside is now equally gripping, with floors themed for the history, industry and artistry of motorized transportation.

CBS Television City   STUDIO

(www.cbs.com; 7800 Beverly Blvd, Los Angeles) North of the Farmers Market is CBS, where game shows, talk shows, soap operas and other programs are taped, often before a live audience, including the *Late Late Show with James Corden, Real Time with Bill Maher* and the perennially popular *Price is Right* game show. Check online for tickets.

⊙ Downtown

Walt Disney Concert Hall   NOTABLE BUILDING

(Map p102; ☑323-850-2000; www.laphil.org; 111 S Grand Ave; ⊙guided tours usually noon & 1:15pm

Thu-Sat, 10am & 11am Sun; P; M Red/Purple Lines to Civic Center/Grand Park) FREE A molten blend of steel, music and psychedelic architecture, this iconic concert venue is the home base of the Los Angeles Philharmonic, but has also hosted contemporary bands such as Phoenix and classic jazz men such as Sonny Rollins. Frank Gehry pulled out all the stops: the building is a gravity-defying sculpture of heaving and billowing stainless steel.

Broad   MUSEUM
(Map p102; ☎213-232-6200; www.thebroad.org; 221 S Grand Ave; ⊘11am-5pm Tue & Wed, to 8pm Thu & Fri, 10am-8pm Sat, to 6pm Sun; P ⊞; M Red/Purple Lines to Civic Center/Grand Park) FREE From the instant it opened in September 2015, the Broad (rhymes with 'road') became a must-visit for contemporary-art fans. It houses the world-class collection of local philanthropist and billionaire real-estate honcho Eli Broad and his wife Edythe, with more than 2000 postwar pieces by dozens of heavy hitters, including Cindy Sherman, Jeff Koons,

Andy Warhol, Roy Lichtenstein, Robert Rauschenberg, Keith Haring and Kara Walker.

MOCA Grand   MUSEUM
(Museum of Contemporary Art; Map p102; ☎213-626-6222; www.moca.org; 250 S Grand Ave; adult/child $15/free, 5-8pm Thu free; ⊘11am-6pm Mon, Wed & Fri, to 8pm Thu, to 5pm Sat & Sun) MOCA's superlative art collection focuses mainly on works created from the 1940s to the present. There's no shortage of luminaries, among them Mark Rothko, Dan Flavin, Willem de Kooning, Joseph Cornell and David Hockney, their creations housed in a postmodern building by award-winning Japanese architect Arata Isozaki. Galleries are below ground, yet sky-lit bright.

Tours

Paramount Pictures   TOURS
(☎323-956-1777; www.paramountstudiotour.com; 5555 Melrose Ave; tours from $55; ⊘tours 9:30am-5pm, last tour 3pm) *Star Trek, Indiana Jones* and *Shrek* are among the blockbusters that originated at Paramount, the country's

---

LA YOGA

Los Angeles enjoys one of the richest and deepest yoga traditions in the West, because this was where the gurus first brought forth their peaceful-warrior wisdom from the ashrams of India.

Parmanahansa Yogananda was one of the first to make the Stateside sojourn, when he came straight from Ranchi, India to address a religious conference in 1920. Three years later the *Los Angeles Times* reported on 'the extraordinary spectacle of thousands...being turned away an hour before the advertised opening of [his] lecture with the 3000-seat LA Philharmonic Hall filled to its utmost capacity.' In October 1925 he established the Self Realization Fellowship at a vacant Mt Washington hotel.

Another powerful guru, Yogi Bhajan, a devout Sikh, arrived here during the second wave, when the American streets were alive with revolution and free love. His classes filled up quickly, especially those at a dusty antique shop on Robertson Blvd, where every night 80 to 90 hippies emerged from packed vans to take his class. Yogi Bhajan told his obviously experimental students, 'Do Kundalini yoga. You can get higher, it's legal and there are no side effects.' One of his original students, Guru Singh, still teaches in town at Yoga West (☎310-552-4647; www.yogawestla.com; 1535 S Robertson Blvd, Mid-City; classes $17; ⊘8:30am-2:30pm & 5-9:30pm Mon, Tue & Thu, 6:45am-2:30pm & 5-9:30pm Wed, 6:45am-2:30pm & 5-8:30pm Fri, 8am-2:30pm Sat, 9:30-noon & 4:30-8:30pm Sun).

Kundalini yoga is but one of many forms offered at yoga studios across LA. The most popular style in town is Hatha yoga, whose original LA pioneer was the Russia-born, India-educated Indra Devi. She opened her Hollywood studio in 1947, teaching the first in a long line of celebrities how to down dog properly. Of course, it just wouldn't be LA without some unexpected offerings in the mix. Among the the best are Vinyasa yoga classes to hip-hop and R&B beats at WeHo studio Y7 (www.y7-studio.com), happy-hour yoga at Arts District cafe The Springs (Map p102; ☎213-223-6226; www.thespringsla.com; 608 Mateo St; lunch $11-15; ⊘7am-8pm Mon-Fri, 9am-6pm Sat & Sun; P ⊜ ⊘), and beer-and-yoga Sunday sessions at nearby Angel City Brewery (Map p102; ☎213-622-1261; www.angelcitybrewery.com; 216 S Alameda St; ⊘4pm-1am Mon-Thu, to 2am Fri, noon-2am Sat, noon-1am Sun).

Downtown Los Angeles

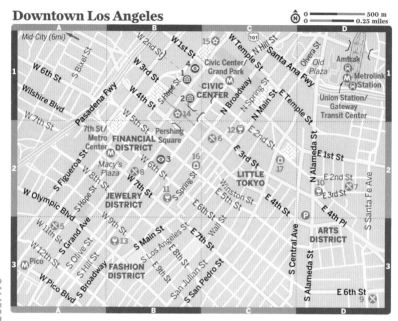

second-oldest movie studio and the only one still in Hollywood proper. Two-hour tours of the studio complex are offered year-round, taking in the back lots and sound stages. Guides are usually passionate and knowledgeable, offering fascinating insights into the studio's history and the movie-making process in general.

On Friday and Saturday nights, Paramount Pictures also runs an After Dark tour (2½ hours), which includes a glass of sparkling wine and snacks. In the fall, this tour also usually includes a walk through the adjacent Hollywood Forever Cemetery, complete with scandalous Hollywood anecdotes. Parking ($12) is available across the street, on the corner of Melrose Ave and Windsor Blvd. Parking is free for those on the VIP or After Dark tours.

Los Angeles Conservancy　WALKING
(☏213-623-2489; www.laconservancy.org; adult/child $15/10) Downtown LA's intriguing historical and architectural gems – from an art-deco penthouse to a beaux-arts ballroom and a dazzling silent-movie theater – are revealed on this nonprofit group's 2½-hour walking tours. To see some of LA's grand historic movie theaters from the inside, the conservancy also offers the Last Remaining

Seats film series, screening classic movies in gilded theaters.

Esotouric BUS

(☑ 213-915-8687; www.esotouric.com; tours $58) Discover LA's lurid and fascinating underbelly on these offbeat, insightful and entertaining walking and bus tours themed around famous crime sites (Black Dahlia anyone?), literary lions (Chandler to Bukowski) and more.

🛏 Sleeping

From rock-and-roll Downtown digs to fabled Hollywood hideaways, LA serves up a dizzying array of slumber options. The key is to plan well ahead. Do your research and find out which neighborhood is most convenient for your plans and best appeals to your style and interests. Trawl the internet for deals, and consider visiting between January and April, when room rates and occupancy are usually at their lowest (Oscars week aside).

Elaine's Hollywood B&B B&B $

(☑ 323-850-0766; www.elaineshollywoodandbreakfast.com; 1616 N Sierra Bonita Ave, Hollywood; r $120-140; 🅿 🐾 ❄ @ ⚲ ⚘; Ⓜ Red Line to Hollywood & Highland) This B&B offers four rooms in a lovingly restored 1910 bungalow on a quiet street. Your outgoing hosts speak several languages, serve a generous continental breakfast and will happily help you plan your day. Cash only.

Mama Shelter BOUTIQUE HOTEL $$

(Map p98; ☑ 323-785-6666; www.mamashelter.com; 6500 Selma Ave; r from $179; ❄ @ ❄; Ⓜ Red Line to Hollywood/Vine) Hip, affordable Mama Shelter keeps things playful with its lobby gumball machines, foosball table and live streaming of guests' selfies and videos. Standard rooms are small but cool, with quality beds and linen and subway-tiled bathrooms with decent-sized showers. Quirky in-room touches include movie scripts, masks and Apple TVs with free Netflix. The rooftop bar is one of LA's best.

Line Hotel HOTEL $$

(☑ 213-381-7411; www.thelinehotel.com; 3515 Wilshire Blvd; r from $170; 🅿 ❄ @ ❄ ⚘; Ⓜ Purple Line to Wilshire/Normandie) Behind the Line is Roy Choi, the man who sparked the LA food-truck revolution and became a celebrity chef. Interiors are sleek and industrial: think (slightly chipped) concrete walls, quirky art-

works and floor-to-ceiling windows overlooking the city. Bathrooms are spotless and in-room tech allows smartphones and music players to be plugged into the flat-screen TV and sound system.

Montage HOTEL $$$

(☑ 888-860-0788; www.montagebeverlyhills.com; 225 N Canon Dr, Beverly Hills; r/ste from $695/1175; 🅿 @ ❄ ⚘) Drawing on-point eye candy and serious wealth, the 201-room Montage balances elegance with warmth and affability. Models and moguls lunch by the gorgeous rooftop pool, while the property's sprawling five-star spa is a Moroccan-inspired marvel, with both single-sex and unisex plunge pools. Rooms are classically styled, with custom Sealy mattresses, dual marble basins, spacious showers and deep-soaking tubs.

Malibu Beach Inn INN $$$

(☑ 310-651-7777; www.malibubeachinn.com; 22878 Pacific Coast Hwy, Malibu; r from $595; 🅿 ❄ ❄) This intimate, adult-oriented hacienda was given a four-star upgrade by Waldo Hernandez, celebrity designer who has done work for the likes of the former Brangelina. The look is ocean-friendly grays and blues, and you might just find yourself face-to-face with well-curated art pieces by the likes of Jasper Johns, Robert Indiana and Andy Warhol.

Its 47 ocean-facing rooms are sheathed in soothing sea colors and outfitted with fireplaces, plush linens, futuristic Japanese toilets and private balconies or terraces. First-floor oceanfront rooms have a deck so close to the beach you can almost touch the rocks. Overnight parking is $35.

Because the beach is private you can take booze from your beach chair.

✕ Eating

✕ Hollywood

Hyperactive Hollywood Blvd is home to a plethora of casual eateries, most of them touristy and mediocre. Clued-in locals tend to gravitate to Highland Ave, where you'll find a handful of great midrange eateries, including Salt's Cure and La Carmencita at the intersection of Lexington Ave, and Petit Trois and Osteria Mozza at the intersection of Melrose Ave. Melrose Ave itself is home to LA's highly acclaimed fine-dining superstar, Providence.

DISNEYLAND & DISNEY CALIFORNIA ADVENTURE

Since opening his Disneyland home in 1955, Mickey has been a thoughtful host to millions of guests. 2001 brought even more visitors to a sister theme park, Disney California Adventure (DCA), just across the plaza. Downtown Disney (which also opened in 2001) offers adventures in shopping and dining for before, during or after parks.

Disneyland Resort is open 365 days a year. During peak summer season, Disneyland's hours are usually 8am to midnight; the rest of the year, it's 10am to 8pm or 10pm. DCA closes at 10pm or 11pm in summer, and earlier in the off-season.

Disneyland

Spotless, wholesome Disneyland is still laid out according to Walt's original plans. It's here you'll find plenty of rides and some of the attractions most associated with the Disney name – Main Street USA, Sleeping Beauty Castle and Tomorrowland.

Main Street USA, gateway to the park, is a pretty thoroughfare lined with old-fashioned Americana ice-cream parlors and shops. Though kids will make a beeline for the rides, adults may enjoy lingering on Main Street for the antique photos and history exhibit just inside the main park entrance at Great Moments with Mr Lincoln (https://disneyland. disney.go.com/attractions/disneyland/disneyland-story; Main Street USA; 🛦).

At the far end of the street is Sleeping Beauty Castle (https://disneyland.disney.go.com/ attractions/disneyland/sleeping-beauty-castle-walkthrough; 🛦), an obligatory photo op and a central landmark worth noting – its towering blue turrets are visible from many areas of the park. The different sections of Disneyland radiate from here like spokes on a wheel.

Disney California Adventure

Across the plaza from Disneyland's monument to fantasy and make-believe is Disney California Adventure (DCA), an ode to California's geography, history and culture – or at least a sanitized G-rated version. DCA, which opened in 2001, covers more acres than Disneyland and feels less crowded, and it has more modern rides and attractions inspired by coastal amusement parks, the inland mountains and redwood forests, the magic of Hollywood, and car culture by way of the movie *Cars*.

Stout Burgers & Beers BURGERS $
(Map p98; ☑ 323-469-3801; www.stoutburgers andbeers.com; 1544 N Cahuenga Blvd; burgers $11-13, salads $8-12; ⏰ 11:30am-4am; 🅿 🛜 ☑; Ⓜ Red Line to Hollywood/Vine) Cool, casual Stout flips gourmet burgers and pours great craft brews. The beef is ground in-house, the chicken is organic and the veggie patties are made fresh daily. One of our favorites here is the Six Weeker, a beef-patty burger jammed with brie, fig jam, arugula and caramelized onions.

Petit Trois FRENCH $$
(☑ 323-468-8916; http://petittrois.com; mains $14-36; ⏰ noon-10pm Sun-Thu, to 11pm Fri & Sat; 🅿) Good things come in small packages... like tiny, no-reservations Petit Trois! Owned by acclaimed TV chef Ludovic Lefebvre, its two long counters (the place is too small for tables) are where food-lovers squeeze in for smashing, honest, Gallic-inspired grub, from a ridiculously light Boursin-stuffed omelet to a showstopping double cheeseburger

served with a standout foie gras–infused red-wine bordelaise.

Musso & Frank Grill STEAK $$
(Map p98; ☑ 323-467-7788; www.mussoand frank.com; 6667 Hollywood Blvd; mains $15-52; ⏰ 11am-11pm Tue-Sat, 4-9pm Sun; 🅿; Ⓜ Red Line to Hollywood/Highland) Hollywood history hangs in the thick air at Musso & Frank Grill, Tinseltown's oldest eatery (since 1919). Charlie Chaplin used to knock back vodka gimlets, Raymond Chandler penned scripts in the high-backed booths, and movie deals were made on the old phone at the back (the booth closest to the phone is favored by Jack Nicholson and Johnny Depp).

Salt's Cure MODERN AMERICAN $$
(☑ 323-465-7258; http://saltscure.com; 1155 N Highland Ave; mains $17-34; ⏰ 11am-11pm Mon-Thu, to midnight Fri, 10am-midnight Sat, 10am-11pm Sun) Wood-paneled, concrete-floored Salt's Cure is an out, proud locavore. From the in-season vegetables to the house-butchered and cured meats, the menu celebrates all things Cali-

DCA's entrance was designed to look like an old-fashioned painted-collage postcard. After passing under the Golden Gate Bridge, you'll arrive at a homage to a 1920s Los Angeles streetscape, complete with a red trolley running down the street.

Plan Your Trip

Disneyland mobile app The most useful tool is Disneyland and Disney California Adventure's official smartphone app, which lets you purchase tickets, make dining reservations, view wait times and locate your favorite characters.

MousePlanet (www.mouseplanet.com) One-stop fansite for all things Disney, with news updates, podcasts, trip reports, reviews and discussion boards.

Theme Park Insider (www.themeparkinsider.com) Newsy blog, travel tips and user reviews of Disneyland rides, attractions and lodging.

Touring Plans (https://touringplans.com) The 'unofficial guide to Disneyland' since 1985. No-nonsense advice, a crowd calendar and a 'lines app.'

Getting There

Disneyland Resort is just off I-5 (Santa Ana Fwy), about 30 miles southeast of Downtown LA. Take the Disneyland Dr exit if you're coming from the north, or the Katella Ave/Disney Way exit from the south.

Arriving at Disneyland Resort is like arriving at an airport. Giant, easy-to-read overhead signs indicate which ramps you need to take for the theme parks, hotels or Anaheim's streets.

All-day parking at Disneyland Resort costs $20 ($25 for oversized vehicles). Enter the 'Mickey & Friends' parking structure from southbound Disneyland Dr, off Ball Rd. Walk outside and follow the signs to board the free tram to Downtown Disney and the theme parks. The parking garage opens one hour before the parks do.

Downtown Disney parking is reserved for diners, shoppers and movie-goers. It has a different rate structure, with the first two hours free and $6 per half-hour thereafter, to a maximum of $36.

fornian. Expect sophisticated takes on rustic comfort grub, whether it's capicollo with chili paste or tender duck breast paired with impressively light oatmeal griddle cakes and blackberry compote.

Providence MODERN AMERICAN $$$
(☑323-460-4170; www.providencela.com; 5955 Melrose Ave; lunch mains $40-45, tasting menus $120-250; ☺noon-2pm & 6-10pm Mon-Fri, 5:30-10pm Sat, 5:30-9pm Sun; P) The top restaurant pick by preeminent LA food critic Jonathan Gold for four years running, this two-starred Michelin darling turns superlative seafood into arresting, nuanced dishes that might see abalone paired with eggplant, turnip and nori, or spiny lobster conspire decadently with macadamia nut and earthy black truffle. À la carte options are available at lunch only.

Osteria & Pizzeria Mozza ITALIAN $$$
(☑osteria 323-297-0100, pizzeria 323-297-0101; http://la.osteriamozza.com; 6602 Melrose Ave; pizzas $11-25, osteria mains $29-38; ☺pizzeria noon-midnight, osteria 5:30-11pm Mon-Fri, 5-11pm Sat, 5-10pm Sun; P) Osteria Mozza crafts fine cuisine from market-fresh, seasonal ingredients, but being a Mario Batali joint, you can expect adventure – think squid-ink chitarra freddi with Dungeness crab, sea urchin and jalapeño – and consistent excellence. Reservations are recommended. Next door, Pizzeria Mozza is a more laid-back and cheaper option, its gorgeous thin-crust pies topped with combos such as squash blossoms, tomato and creamy burrata.

✖ Los Feliz & Griffith Park

Los Feliz has a vibrant dining scene that will have you chowing everything from Texan breakfast tacos and Yucatecan tamales to French pastries, smoky ribs, contemporary Middle Eastern skate plates and cult-status, seasonally inspired ice cream. The scene is focused on Vermont and Highland Aves, with a burgeoning scene now luring diners on Hollywood Blvd between the two.

In Griffith Park, outdoor Trails is a popular lunch spot for hikers.

Jeni's Splendid Ice Creams
ICE CREAM $

(☎323-928-2668; https://jenis.com; 1954 Hillhurst Ave, Los Feliz; 2/3/4 flavors $5.50/6.50/7.50; ☺11am-11pm) Rarely short of a queue, this Ohio import scoops some of the city's creamiest, most inventive ice cream. Forget plain vanilla. Here, signature flavors include brown butter almond brittle and a riesling-poached-pear sorbet. Then there are the limited-edition offerings, which might leave you tossing up between a juniper and lemon-curd combo, or a spicy Queen City Cayenne. Tough gig.

HomeState
TEX-MEX $

(☎323-906-1122; www.myhomestate.com; 4624 Hollywood Blvd, Los Feliz; tacos $3.50, dishes $7-10; ☺8am-3pm; Ⓜ Red Line to Vermont/Sunset) Texan expat Briana Valdez is behind this rustic ode to the Lone Star State. Locals queue patiently for authentic breakfast tacos such as the Trinity, a handmade flour tortilla topped with egg, bacon, potato and cheddar. Then there's the *queso* (melted cheese) and our lunchtime favorite, the brisket sandwich, a coaxing combo of tender meat, cabbage slaw, guacamole and pickled jalapeños in pillow-soft white bread.

Mess Hall
PUB FOOD $$

(☎323-660-6377; www.messhallkitchen.com; 4500 Los Feliz Blvd, Los Feliz; mains $16-35; ☺9am-

Hollywood Sign (p97)
NITO / SHUTTERSTOCK ©

10pm Sun-Thu, to 11pm Fri & Sat; Ⓟⓢ) What was formerly The Brown Derby, a swing dance spot made famous by the film *Swingers,* is now a handsome, cabin-style hangout with snug booths, TV sports and a comfy, neighborly vibe. The feel-good factor extends to the menu, with standouts that include comforting mac-n-cheese and smoky baby-back ribs with slaw and house fries.

✖ Beverly Hills, Bel Air, Brentwood & Westwood

B Sweet Dessert Bar
DESSERTS $

(☎310-963-9769; www.mybsweet.com; 2005 Sawtelle Blvd; desserts from $5; ☺noon-11pm Wed-Sat, to 8pm Sun) Dessert fans flock to this hip, adorable storefront in Sawtelle Japantown for its weekly-changing selection of bread pudding from over 40 flavors: maple bacon, chocolate doughnut, salted caramel etc. Then there's the halo, an ice-cream sandwich pressed like hot panini inside a glazed doughnut...mercy! Get yours with coffee and teas on tap, or brownies from 'fudgiest' to 'sluttiest.'

Joss Cuisine
CHINESE $$

(☎310-277-3888; www.josscuisine.com; 9919 S Santa Monica Blvd, Beverly Hills; dishes $15-30; ☺noon-3pm Mon-Fri, 5:30-10pm daily) With fans including Barbra Streisand, Gwenyth Paltrow and Jackie Chan, this warm, intimate nosh spot serves up superlative, MSG-free Chinese cuisine at noncelebrity prices. Premium produce drives a menu of exceptional dishes, from flawless dim sum and ginger fish broth to crispy mustard prawns and one of the finest Peking ducks you'll encounter this side of East Asia. Reservations recommended.

✖ West Hollywood & Mid-City

Night + Market
THAI $

(☎310-275-9724; www.nightmarketla.com; 9043 W Sunset Blvd, West Hollywood; dishes $8-15; ☺11:30am-2:30pm Tue-Thu, 5-10:30pm Tue-Sun) Set behind Talésai, a long-running Thai joint, this related kitchen pumps out outstanding Thai street food and Thai-inspired hybrids such as catfish tamales. Pique the appetite with *larb lanna* (chopped pork salad), push the envelope with rich *pork toro* (grilled pork collar) then move onto winners like *chiengrei* herb sausage and a pad Thai that makes standard LA versions seem overly sweet.

LOS ANGELES FOOD TRUCKS

Any LA foodie will tell you that some of the best bites in town come on four wheels. Food trucks are no less popular here than in any other cool, food-loving metropolis, with their mobile kitchens serving up a global feast of old- and new-school flavors. You can track food trucks at Roaming Hunger (www.roaminghunger.com), or check the websites, Twitter or Instagram feeds of the following LA favorites. All trucks listed below accept credit cards.

Free Range (www.freerangela.com) Famed for its signature tempura-fried chicken with Fresno-chili slaw and honey mustard sauce, jammed into a toasted Portuguese bun.

Yeasty Boys (http://yeastieboysbagels.com) Fluffy-centered, hand-rolled bagels available in plain, poppy, sesame cheddar and everything.

Kogi BBQ (http://kogibbq.com) Chef Roy Choi is a founding dude of the LA food-truck scene and his four trucks (Roja, Verde, Naranja and Rosita) peddle standout Korean-Mexican fusion fare.

Plant Food for People (http://pffp.org) Smashing plant-based street food good enough for herbivores *and* omnivores.

Guerrilla Tacos (www.guerrillatacos.com) Chef Wes Avila brings his fine-dining background to his blue-hued truck, which offers an oft-tweaked, seasonal Mexican menu using quality, sustainable produce from local farms and artisanal purveyors.

Ta Bom Truck (www.tabomtruck.com) Take one mom from Sao Paolo, add two daughters and a shared passion for Brazilian food and, presto, you get Ta Bom.

Crossroads
VEGAN $$

(📞 323-782-9245; www.crossroadskitchen.com; 8284 Melrose Ave, Mid-City; brunch mains $7-14, dinner mains $12-22; ⊙10am-2pm daily, 5-10pm Sun-Thu, to midnight Fri & Sat; 🖋) Tal Ronnen didn't get to be a celebrity chef (Oprah, Ellen) by serving ordinary vegan fare. Instead, seasonal creations include 'crab cakes' made from hearts of palm, artichoke 'oysters' and porcini-crusted eggplant, alongside pizzas and pastas incorporating innovative nut 'cheeses.' Leave the Birkenstocks at home; this place is sophisticated, with full bar and cool cocktails.

Gracias Madre
VEGAN, MEXICAN $$

(📞 323-978-2170; www.graciasmadreweho.com; 8905 Melrose Ave, West Hollywood; mains lunch $10-13, dinner $12-18; ⊙11am-11pm Mon-Fri, from 10am Sat & Sun; 🖋) Gracias Madre shows just how tasty – and chichi – organic, plant-based Mexican cooking can be. Sit on the gracious patio or in the cozy interior and feel good as you eat healthily: sweet-potato flautas, coconut 'bacon' and plantain 'quesadillas,' plus salads and bowls. We're consistently surprised at innovations like cashew 'cheese,' mushroom 'chorizo' and jackfruit 'carnitas.'

Republique
BISTRO $$$

(📞 310-362-6115; www.republiquela.com; 624 S La Brea Ave, Mid-City; mains lunch $11-19, dinner $14-56; ⊙8am-4pm daily, 5:30-10pm Sun-Thu, to 11pm Fri & Sat; 🅿🚻; 🚇MTA line 20, 720) A design gem with the gourmet ambition to match. The old interior of LA's dearly departed Campanile is still an atrium restaurant with stone arches, a brightly lit front end scattered with butcher-block tables, and a marble bar peering into an open kitchen. There are tables in the darker, oakier backroom too.

Connie & Ted's
SEAFOOD $$$

(📞 323-848-2722; www.connieandteds.com; 8171 Santa Monica Blvd, West Hollywood; mains $13-44; ⊙4-10pm Mon & Tue, 11:30am-10pm Wed & Thu, 11:30am-11pm Fri, 10am-11pm Sat, 10am-10pm Sun; 🅿) At this modernized version of a New England seafood shack by acclaimed chef Michael Cimarusti, there are always up to a dozen oyster varieties at the raw bar, classics such as fried clams, grilled fish (wild and sustainably raised), lobsters and steamers, lobster rolls served cold with mayo or hot with drawn butter, and shellfish marinara is a sacred thing.

✕ Downtown

The DTLA dining scene is booming and diverse, with an ever-expanding cache of on-trend restaurants and cafes, plus no-fuss cheapies. Hubs include Grand Central Market for fresh, multiculti bites, Little Tokyo for quality ramen and sashimi, Chinatown for Chinese and both the Arts District and the Downtown core for hot-spot bistros and produce-driven menus. Across the LA River, humble Boyle Heights is a top choice for authentic, low-frills Mexican street food.

Manuela   MODERN AMERICAN $$

(Map p102; ☑323-849-0480; www.manuela-la. com; 907 E 3rd St; ⊙5:30-10pm Sun-Thu, to 11pm Fri & Sat, also 11:30am-3:30pm Wed-Fri & 10am-4pm Sat & Sun; 🐾) Young Texan chef Wes Whitsell heads this deserving it-kid inside the Hauser & Wirth complex. The woody warmth of the loft-like space is echoed in the oft-tweaked menu, a beautiful fusion of local ingredients and smoky southern accents. Pique the appetite with a house-pickled appetizer then lose yourself in deceptively simple soul-stirrers like sultry pork ragu over flawless polenta.

Maccheroni Republic   ITALIAN $$

(Map p102; ☑213-346-9725; www.maccheroni republic.com; 332 S Broadway; mains $11-18; ⊙11:30am-2:30pm & 5:30-10pm Mon-Thu, 11:30am-2:30pm & 5:30-10:30pm Fri, 11:30am-10:30pm Sat, 11:30am-9pm Sun) Tucked away on a still-ungentrified corner is this gem with a leafy heated patio and tremendous Italian slow-cooked food. Don't miss the *polpettine di gamberi* (flattened ground shrimp cakes fried in olive oil), and its range of delicious housemade pastas. Perfectly al dente, the pasta is made using organic semolina flour and served with gorgeous crusty bread to mop up the sauce.

Broken Spanish   MEXICAN $$$

(Map p102; ☑213-749-1460; http://brokenspanish. com; 1050 S Flower St; mains $22-49; ⊙5:30-10pm Sun-Thu, to 11pm Fri & Sat; 🐾) Despite retro design nods such as concrete blocks, macrame plant hangers and terracotta lampshades, Ray Garcia's sleek Downtown eatery is all about confident, contemporary Mexican cooking. From the *chochoyoes* (masa dumplings with green garlic and pasilla pepper) to a rich, intense dish of mushrooms with black garlic, flavors are clean and intriguing, and the presentation polished.

Q Sushi   SUSHI $$$

(Map p102; ☑213-225-6285; www.qsushila. com; 521 W 7th St; per person lunch/dinner from $75/165; ⊙noon-1:30pm Tue-Fri, 6-9pm Tue-Sat; 🅿) Sushi and sashimi hit dizzying highs at this *omakase* heavyweight, where bite-sized bliss comes from the likes of tender octopus braised in sake and brown sugar, or blow-torched toro made with rice fermented for a month. Dinner consists of 20 courses (lunch about half that), all created by Japanese sushi savant Hiro Naruke, who lost his business in the post-tsunami aftermath. Reserve ahead.

🍷 Drinking & Nightlife

Whether you're seeking an organic Kurimi espresso, a saison brewed with Chinatown-sourced Oolong tea or a craft cocktail made with peanut-butter-washed Campari LA pours on cue. From post-industrial coffee roasters and breweries to mid-century lounges, classic Hollywood martini bars and cocktail-pouring bowling alleys, LA serves its drinks with a generous splash of wow. So do the right thing and raise your glass to America's finest town.

🍸 Hollywood

Hollywood's bar scene is diverse and delicious, with a large number of venues located on or just off Hollywood Blvd. You'll find everything from historic dive and cocktail bars once frequented by Hollywood legends, to velvet-rope hot spots, buzzing rooftop hotel bars and even a rum-and-cigar hideaway. Some of the more fashionable spots have dress codes or implement reservations-only policies, so always check ahead and prepare accordingly.

Rooftop Bar at Mama Shelter   BAR

(Map p98; ☑323-785-6600; www.mamashelter. com/en/los-angeles/restaurants/rooftop; 6500 Selma Ave; ⊙11am-midnight; Ⓜ Red Line to Hollywood/Vine) Less a hotel rooftop bar than a lush, tropical-like oasis with killer views of the Hollywood sign and LA skyline, multi-colored day beds and tongue-in-cheek bar bites like a 'Trump' turkey burger. Pulling everyone from hotel guests to locals from the nearby Buzzfeed and Lulu offices, it's a winning spot for languid cocktail sessions, landmark spotting and a game of Jenga Giant.

Designer shops on Rodeo Drive (p99)

Sassafras Saloon BAR

(☑ 323-467-2800; www.sassafrashollywood.com; 1233 N Vine St; ⊘5pm-2am) You'll be pining for the bayou at the hospitable Sassafras Saloon, where hanging moss and life-size facades evoke sultry Savannah. Cocktails include a barrel-aged Sazerac, while themed nights include live jazz on Sunday and Monday, brass bands and acrobatics on Tuesday, burlesque and blues on Wednesday, karaoke on Thursday, and DJ-spun tunes on Friday and Saturday.

Library Bar COCKTAIL BAR

(Map p98; ☑ 323-769-8888; www.thehollywood-roosevelt.com/about/food-drink/library-bar; Roosevelt Hotel, 7000 Hollywood Blvd; ⊘6pm-1am; 🛜; Ⓜ Red Line to Hollywood/Highland) Evoking an old hunting lodge with its timber panels, Chesterfield sofas and mounted antlers, this handsome hideaway sits off the Roosevelt Hotel's fountain-studded lobby. You won't find a cocktail menu here; simply tell the barkeeps what you're in the mood for and let them work their magic.

📍 Los Feliz & Griffith Park

Dresden COCKTAIL BAR

(☑ 323-665-4294; www.thedresden.com; 1760 N Vermont Ave, Los Feliz; ⊘4:30pm-2am Mon-Sat, to midnight Sun; Ⓜ Red Line to Vermont/Sunset) Marty and Elayne have been a Los Feliz fixture since 1982 when they first brought their quirky Sinatra style to the Dresden's mid-century lounge. He rumbles on the drums and the upright bass; she tickles the ivories and plays the flute. Both sing. Their fame peaked when they made a brief appearance in the film *Swingers*.

Tiki-Ti BAR

(☑ 323-669-9381; www.tiki-ti.com; 4427 W Sunset Blvd; ⊘4pm-2am Wed-Sat) Channeling Waikiki since 1961, this tiny tropical tavern packs in everyone from Gen-Y hipsters to grizzled old-timers in 'non-ironic' Hawaiian shirts. Drinks are strong and smooth; order the tequila-fueled Blood and Sand and expect a ritual that involves raucous cheers and a charging bull. The brown-paper tags are notes written by regulars, some of them dating back to the '60s.

📍 Beverly Hills, Bel Air, Brentwood & Westwood

This part of town is all about cocktails in plush hotel bars. The Polo Lounge at the Beverly Hills Hotel heaves with Hollywood lore, while nightly jazz sessions make the Hotel Bel-Air and Vibrato Grill Bar seductive options. Cocktails at these venues average around $20, though the atmosphere and history make it worth the expense. Collegiate Westwood is a more laid-back affair, with numerous sports bars and laptop-friendly cafes.

109

The original Farmers Market (p100)

Bar & Lounge
at Hotel Bel-Air
COCKTAIL BAR

(📋 310-909-1644; www.dorchestercollection.com/en/los-angeles/hotel-bel-air; Hotel Bel-Air, 701 Stone Canyon Rd, Bel Air; ⏱ 2:30pm-midnight Mon-Thu, to 2am Fri & Sat, 11am-midnight Sun) You'll be clinking crystal at the Hotel Bel-Air's dark, intimate hideaway, a deco-inspired bar-lounge graced with white-marble fireplace and blown-up photography by Norman Seeff. The grand piano is tickled nightly with silky jazz; try catching the fabulous Maria de la Vega Trio on Wednesday nights. Flawless cocktails aside, the bar offers an exceptional food menu by celebrity chef Wolfgang Puck. Style up.

Polo Lounge
COCKTAIL BAR

(📋 310-887-2777; www.dorchestercollection.com/en/los-angeles/the-beverly-hills-hotel; Beverly Hills Hotel, 9641 Sunset Blvd, Beverly Hills; ⏱ 7am-1:30am) For a classic LA experience, dress up and swill martinis in the Beverly Hills Hotel's legendary bar. Charlie Chaplin had a standing lunch reservation at booth one, and it was here that HR Haldeman and John Ehrlichman learned of the Watergate break-in in 1972. There's a popular Sunday jazz brunch (adult/child $75/35).

🍸 West Hollywood & Mid-City

WeHo is party central, especially on Sunset and Santa Monica Blvds. For SoCal's LGBTIQ+ community, Santa Monica Blvd between about Robertson and La Cienega Blvds is also known as Boys Town, complete with rainbow-painted crosswalks – it's super fun and flirty, especially on weekend nights. Off this strip are some of America's best comedy clubs, classic cocktail and tequila bars, and even a cat cafe.

Abbey
LGBTIQ+

(📋 310-289-8410; www.theabbeyweho.com; 692 N Robertson Blvd, West Hollywood; ⏱ 11am-2am Mon-Thu, from 10am Fri, from 9am Sat & Sun) It's been called the best gay bar in the world, and who are we to argue? Once a humble coffee house, the Abbey has expanded into WeHo's bar/club/restaurant of record. Always a party, it has so many different flavored martinis and mojitos that you'd think they were invented here, plus a full menu of upscale pub food (mains $14 to $21).

Crumbs & Whiskers
CAT CAFE

(📋 323-879-9389; www.crumbsandwhiskers.com; 7924 Melrose Ave, Mid-City; 75min visit weekdays/weekends $22/25; ⏱ 11am-7:45pm Thu-Tue; 📶) Humans commune with kitties at LA's first cat cafe. The spare, stylish black-box storefront is kitted out with fluffy futons and climbing shelves, and humans can observe and gently touch felines while drinking coffee and tea. Resident cats were rescued from high-kill shelters and are up for adoption, but here you're in their environment, not the other way around.

🍸 Downtown

Clifton's Republic
COCKTAIL BAR

(Map p102; 📋 213-627-1673; www.cliftonsla.com; 648 S Broadway; ⏱ 11am-midnight Tue-Thu, to 2am Fri, 10am-2:30am Sat, 10am-midnight Sun; 📶; Ⓜ Red/Purple Lines to Pershing Sq) Opened in 1935 and back after a $10-million renovation, multilevel, mixed-crowd Clifton's defies description. You can chow retro-cafeteria classics (meals around $14.75) by a forest waterfall, order drinks from a Gothic church altar, watch burlesque performers shimmy in the shadow of a 40ft faux redwood, or slip through a glass-paneled door to a luxe tiki paradise where DJs spin in a repurposed speedboat.

Edison
COCKTAIL BAR

(Map p102; 📋 213-613-0000; www.edisondowntown.com; 108 W 2nd St; ⏱ 5pm-2am Wed-Fri, from 7pm Sat; Ⓜ Red/Purple Lines to Civic Center/Grand Park) Accessed through easy-to-miss Harlem

Pl alleyway, this extraordinary basement lounge sits in a century-old power plant. It's like a dimly lit, steampunk wonderland, punctuated with vintage generators, handsome leather lounges and secret nooks. Look for celebrity signatures in the original coal furnace and stick around for the live tunes (anything from jazz to folk), burlesque or aerialist performances.

Upstairs at the Ace Hotel   BAR
(Map p102; www.acehotel.com/losangeles; 929 S Broadway, Downtown; ⊙11am-2am) What's not to love about a rooftop bar with knockout Downtown views, powerful cocktails and a luxe, safari-inspired fit out? Perched on the 14th floor of the Ace Hotel, this chilled, sophisticated space has on-point DJs and specially commissioned artworks that include an installation made using Skid Row blankets.

☆ Entertainment

Hollywood Bowl   CONCERT VENUE
(⬚323-850-2000; www.hollywoodbowl.com; 2301 N Highland Ave; rehearsals free, performance costs vary; ⊙Jun-Sep) Summers in LA just wouldn't be the same without alfresco melodies un-

der the stars at the Bowl, a huge natural amphitheater in the Hollywood Hills. Its annual season – which usually runs from June to September – includes symphonies, jazz bands and iconic acts such as Blondie, Bryan Ferry and Angélique Kidjo. Bring a sweater or blanket as it gets cool at night.

Greek Theatre   LIVE MUSIC
(⬚844-524-7335;   www.lagreektheatre.com; 2700 N Vermont Ave; ⊙Apr-Oct) The 'Greek' in the 2010 film *Get Him to the Greek* is this 5900-capacity outdoor amphitheater, tucked into a woodsy Griffith Park hillside. A more intimate version of the Hollywood Bowl, it's much loved for its vibe and variety – recent acts include PJ Harvey, John Legend and Pepe Aguilar. Parking (cash only) is stacked, so plan on a postshow wait.

Saturdays Off the 405   LIVE MUSIC
(www.getty.edu; Getty Center; ⊙6-9pm Sat May-Sep) From May to September, the Getty Center courtyard fills with evening crowds for a delicious collision of art, brilliant live acts and beat-pumping DJ sets.

FREE SUMMER CONCERTS

Summer in LA means free concert series across the city, most of which take place weekly. Toast to long days and soul-lifting tunes at the following standouts.

Twilight Concert Series (p118) Some of the biggest crowds rock up to Santa Monica Pier for a mix of indie pop, rock, reggae, Latin, soul, classical and more, every Thursday from early July to early September.

Saturdays Off the 405 (p111) From May to September, the Getty Center courtyard fills with evening crowds for a delicious collision of art, brilliant live acts and beat-pumping DJ sets.

KCRW Summer Nights (http://summernights.kcrw.com; ⊙Jun-Aug) A popular, weekly concert series popping up at different locations across the city from June to August. DJs, live bands, food trucks, craft beer and art workshops.

Jazz at LACMA (www.lacma.org; 5905 Wilshire Blvd, Mid-City; ⊙6pm Fri) FREE A hugely popular Friday-night series at one of LA's finest art museums, with top-tier jazz acts and open galleries. Runs from April to November.

Grand Performances (Map p102; ⬚213-687-2190; www.grandperformances.org; California Plaza, 300 & 350 S Grand Ave; ⊙Jun-Sep; Ⓜ Red/Purple Lines to Pershing Sq) FREE Serves up local and international music acts on Downtown's California Plaza on Friday and Saturday nights from June to September. Expect everything from world music and hip-hop to theater and other cultural events.

Pershing Square (Map p102; www.laparks.org; 532 S Olive St; Ⓜ) This Downtown square hosts a busy program of cultural events from early July to mid-August. This includes its Saturday-night concert series, featuring anything from Brit dance acts to '80s rock icons.

Upright Citizens Brigade Theatre

COMEDY

(Map p98; 323-908-8702; http://franklin.ucb-theatre.com; 5919 Franklin Ave; tickets $5-12) Founded in New York by *Saturday Night Live* alums Amy Poehler and Ian Roberts along with Matt Besser and Matt Walsh, this sketch-comedy group cloned itself in Hollywood in 2005. With numerous nightly shows spanning anything from stand-up comedy to improv and sketch, it's arguably the best comedy hub in town. Valet parking costs $7.

Geffen Playhouse

THEATER

(310-208-5454; www.geffenplayhouse.com; 10886 Le Conte Ave, Westwood) American magnate and producer David Geffen forked over $17 million to get his Mediterranean-style playhouse back into shape. The center's season includes both American classics and freshly minted works, and it's not unusual to see well-known film and TV actors treading the boards.

Mark Taper Forum

THEATER

(Map p102; 213-628-2772; www.centertheatregroup.org; 135 N Grand Ave) Part of the Music Center, the Mark Taper is one of the three venues used by the Center Theatre Group, SoCal's leading resident ensemble and producer of Tony-, Pulitzer- and Emmy-winning plays. It's an intimate space with only 15 rows of seats arranged around a thrust stage, so you can see every sweat pearl on the actors' faces.

Comedy Store

COMEDY

(323-650-6268; www.thecomedystore.com; 8433 W Sunset Blvd, West Hollywood) There's no comedy club in the city with more street cred than Sammy and Mitzi Shore's Comedy Store on the strip. Sammy launched the club, but Mitzi was the one who brought in hot young comics such as Richard Pryor, George Carlin, Eddie Murphy, Robin Williams and David Letterman. There are three stages, meaning something's on just about every night.

Shopping

Skylight Books

BOOKS

(323-660-1175; www.skylightbooks.com; 1818 N Vermont Ave, Los Feliz; 10am-10pm) Occupying two adjoining shopfronts, this much-loved Los Feliz institution carries everything from art, architecture and fashion tomes, to LA history titles, vegan cookbooks, queer literature and critical theory. There's a solid selection of niche magazines and local zines, some great lit-themed tees and regular, engaging in-store readings and talks (with the podcasts uploaded onto the store's website).

Mystery Pier Books

BOOKS

(www.mysterypierbooks.com; 8826 W Sunset Blvd, West Hollywood; 11am-7pm Mon-Sat, noon-5pm Sun) An intimate, hidden-away courtyard shop that specializes in selling signed shooting scripts from past blockbusters, and first editions from Shakespeare ($2500 to

Frank Gehry–designed Walt Disney Concert Hall (p100)

FLEA MARKET STANDOUTS

Flea markets are like urban archaeology: you'll need plenty of patience and luck when sifting through other people's trash and detritus, but oh, the thrill when you finally unearth a treasure! Arrive early, bring small bills, wear walking shoes and get ready to haggle. These are the best of the best.

Rose Bowl Flea Market (www.rgcshows.com; 1001 Rose Bowl Dr, Pasadena; admission from $9; ⊙9am-4:30pm 2nd Sun each month, last entry 3pm, early admission from 5am) Pasadena's massive monthly Sunday market draws hunters and collectors from across the US.

Melrose Trading Post (www.melrosetradingpost.org; Fairfax High School, 7850 Melrose Ave, Mid-City; admission $3; ⊙9am-5pm Sun; ⊡MTA lines 217, 218, 10) Held at Fairfax High School, this is one of LA's trendiest secondhand hot spots, with vintage furniture, decorative objects, fashion, accessories and more.

Pasadena City College Flea Market (www.pasadena.edu; 1570 E Colorado Blvd, Pasadena; ⊙8am-3pm 1st Sun of each month) The Rose Bowl's free, less-hyped sibling, with fashion, accessories, crafts and an especially notable selection of vinyl.

$4000), Salinger ($21,000) and JK Rowling ($30,000 and up).

Last Bookstore in Los Angeles   BOOKS
(Map p102; ☑213-488-0599; www.lastbookstore
la.com; 453 S Spring St; ⊙10am-10pm Mon-Thu, to 11pm Fri & Sat, to 9pm Sun) What started as a one-man operation out of a Main St storefront is now California's largest new-and-used bookstore, spanning two levels of an old bank building. Eye up the cabinets of rare books before heading upstairs, home to a horror-and-crime book den, a book tunnel and a few art galleries to boot. The store also houses a terrific vinyl collection.

Raggedy Threads   VINTAGE
(Map p102; ☑213-620-1188; www.raggedythreads.
com; 330 E 2nd St; ⊙noon-8pm Mon-Sat, to 6pm Sun; ⓂGold Line to Little Tokyo/Arts District) A tremendous vintage Americana store just off the main Little Tokyo strip. There's plenty of beautifully ragged denim, with a notable collection of pre-1950s workwear from the US, Japan and France. You'll also find a good number of Victorian dresses, soft T-shirts and a wonderful turquoise collection at decent prices.

Reformation   FASHION & ACCESSORIES
(www.thereformation.com; 8253 Melrose Ave, Mid-City; ⊙11am-7pm Mon-Sat, to 6pm Sun) ∥ Here's classic, retro-inspired, fashionable women's wear that's eco-conscious without the granola. It does it by using pre-existing materials, which means no additional dyeing of fabrics and half the water use of other fashion brands, and with an eye toward minimizing

waste from sourcing to production, sales and even recycling. Everything is made locally.

Fred Segal   FASHION & ACCESSORIES
(☑323-651-4129; www.fredsegal.com; 8100 Melrose Ave, Mid-City; ⊙10am-7pm Mon-Sat, noon-6pm Sun) Celebs and beautiful people circle for the very latest from Babakul, Aviator Nation and Robbi & Nikki at this warren of high-end boutiques under one impossibly chic but slightly snooty roof. The only time you'll see bargains (sort of) is during the two-week blowout sale in September.

Wasteland   VINTAGE
(www.shopwasteland.com; 7428 Melrose Ave, Mid-City; ⊙11am-8pm Mon-Sat, from noon Sun) Large, popular and rather-polished vintage boutique with racks packed with skirts and tops, fur-collared jackets and Pendleton wool shirts.

Book Soup   BOOKS
(☑310-659-3110; www.booksoup.com; 8818 W Sunset Blvd, West Hollywood; ⊙9am-10pm Mon-Sat, to 7pm Sun) A bibliophile's indie gem, sprawling and packed with entertainment, travel, feminist and queer studies, and eclectic and LA-based fiction, with appearances by big-name authors.

Grove   MALL
(☑323-900-8080; www.thegrovela.com; 189 The Grove Dr; ⊙10am-9pm Mon-Thu, to 10pm Fri & Sat, to 8pm Sun; ⊡MTA line 16) This faux Italian palazzo is one of LA's most popular shopping destinations, with 40 name-brand stores, a fountain and a trolley rolling down the middle.

Venice Beach, Santa Monica

❶ Information

Los Angeles Visitor Information Center (Map p98; ✆ 323-467-6412; www.discoverlos angeles.com; Hollywood & Highland, 6801 Hollywood Blvd; ⊙ 8am-10pm Mon-Sat, 9am-7pm Sun; Ⓜ Red Line to Hollywood/Highland) The main tourist office for Los Angeles, located in Hollywood. Maps, brochures and lodging information, plus tickets to theme parks and attractions.

❶ Getting Around

Unless time is no factor – or money is extremely tight – you're going to want to spend some time behind the wheel, although this means contending with some of the worst traffic in the country. Avoid rush hour (7am to 9am and 3:30pm to 6pm).

Most public transportation is handled by **Metro** (✆ 323-466-3876; www.metro.net), which offers maps, schedules and trip-planning help through its website.

To ride Metro trains and buses, buy a reusable TAP card. Available from TAP vending machines at Metro stations with a $1 surcharge, the cards allow you to add a preset cash value or day passes. The regular base fare is $1.75 per boarding, or $7 for a day pass with unlimited rides. Both single-trip tickets and TAP cards loaded with a day pass are available on Metro buses (ensure you have the exact change). When using a TAP card, tap the card against the sensor at station entrances and aboard buses.

TAP cards are accepted on DASH and municipal bus services and can be reloaded at vending machines or online on the TAP website (www.taptogo.net).

SANTA MONICA

Santa Monica is LA's cute, alluring, hippy-chic little sister, its karmic counterbalance and, to many, its salvation. Surrounded by LA on three sides and the Pacific on the fourth, SaMo is a place where real-life Lebowskis sip White Russians next to martini-swilling Hollywood producers, celebrity chefs dine at family-owned taque-rias, and soccer moms and career bachelors shop at abundant farmers markets. All the while, kids, out-of-towners and those who love them flock to wide beaches and the pier, where the landmark Ferris wheel and roller coaster welcome one and all.

⊙ Sights

Santa Monica Pier   LANDMARK
(✆ 310-458-8901; www.santamonicapier.org; ⓘ) Once the very end of the mythic Route 66, and still the object of a tourist love affair, the Santa Monica Pier dates back to 1908 and is the city's most compelling landmark. There are arcades, carnival games, a vintage carousel, a Ferris wheel, a roller coaster and an aquarium, and the pier comes alive with free concerts (Twilight Dance Series) and outdoor movies in the summertime.

There are also a number of bars and restaurants, but the thing here is the view: the pier extends almost a quarter-mile over the Pacific, so you can stroll to the edge, hang out among the motley anglers and lose yourself in the rolling, blue-green sea.

Kids get their kicks at **Pacific Park** (☑310-260-8744; www.pacpark.com; 380 Santa Monica Pier; per ride $5-10, all-day pass adult/child under 8yr $32/18; ☉daily, seasonal hours vary; ⊞; Ⓜ Expo Line to Downtown Santa Monica), a small amusement park with a solar-powered Ferris wheel, kiddy rides, midway games and food stands. Check the website for discount coupons.

Near the pier entrance, nostalgic souls and their offspring can giddy up the beautifully hand-painted horses of the 1922 **carousel** (☑310-394-8042; Santa Monica Pier; ☉hours vary; ⊞), also featured in the movie *The Sting*.

Peer under the pier – just below the carousel – for Heal the Bay's **Santa Monica Pier Aquarium** (☑310-393-6149; www.healthe bay.org; 1600 Ocean Front Walk; adult/child $5/free; ☉2-6pm Tue-Fri, 12:30-6pm Sat & Sun; ⊞; Ⓜ Expo Line to Downtown Santa Monica) ⬦. Sea stars, crabs, sea urchins and other critters and crustaceans scooped from the bay stand by to be petted – ever so gently – in their touch-tank homes.

South of the pier is the **Original Muscle Beach** (www.musclebeach.net; 1800 Ocean Front Walk; ☉sunrise-sunset), where the Southern California exercise craze began in the mid-20th century. New equipment now draws a fresh generation of fitness fanatics. Close by, the search for the next Bobby Fischer is on at the International Chess Park (p115). Anyone can join in. Following the **South Bay Bicycle Trail** (☉sunrise-sunset; ⊞), a paved bike and walking path, south for about 1.5 miles takes you straight to Venice Beach. Bike or in-line skates are available to rent on the pier and at beachside kiosks.

Santa Monica State Beach   BEACH
(☑310-458-8411; www.smgov.net/portals/beach; ☐Big Blue Bus 1) There are endless ways to enjoy this 3.5-mile stretch of sand, running from Venice Beach in the south to Will Rogers State Beach in the north. Sunbathing and swimming are obvious options, but you can also reserve time on a beach volleyball court or, for more cerebral pursuits, settle in at a first-come first-served chess table at **International Chess Park** (☑310-458-8450; www.smgov.net; Ocean Front Walk at Seaside Tce; ☉sunrise-sunset), just south of the Santa Monica pier.

Palisades Park   PARK
(☑800-544-5319; Ocean Ave btwn Colorado Ave & San Vicente Blvd; ☉5am-midnight) **FREE** Perhaps it's appropriate that Route 66, America's most romanticized byway, ends at this

---

VENICE BOARDWALK

Life in Venice moves to a different rhythm and nowhere more so than on the famous Venice Boardwalk, officially known as Ocean Front Walk. It's a freak show, a human zoo and a wacky carnival alive with Hula-hoop magicians, old-timey jazz combos, solo distorted garage rockers and artists (good and bad) – as far as LA experiences go, it's a must.

Murals

Venice Beach has long been associated with street art, and for decades there was a struggle between outlaw artists and law enforcement. Art won out and the tagged-up towers and the free-standing concrete wall of the **Venice Beach Art Walls** (www. veniceartwalls.com; 1800 Ocean Front Walk, Venice; ☉10am-5pm Sat & Sun; ⊞), right on the beach, have been covered by graffiti artists from 1961 to the present.

Muscle Beach

Gym rats with an exhibitionist streak can get a tan and a workout at this famous outdoor **gym** (☑310-399-2775; www.musclebeach.net; 1800 Ocean Front Walk, Venice; per day $10; ☉8am-7pm Mon-Sat, 10am-4pm Sun Apr-Sep, shorter hours rest of year) right on the Venice Boardwalk, where Arnold Schwarzenegger and Franco Columbu once bulked up.

Venice Skatepark

Long the destination of local skate punks, the concrete at this **skate park** (www.venice skatepark.com; 1500 Ocean Front Walk, Venice; ☉dawn-dusk) has now been molded and steel-fringed into 17,000 sq ft of vert, tranny and street terrain with unbroken ocean views. The old-school-style skate run and the world-class pool are most popular for high flyers and gawking spectators. Great photo ops, especially as the sun sets.

Santa Monica & Venice

gorgeous cliffside park perched dramatically on the edge of the continent. Stretching 1.5 miles north from the pier, this palm-dotted greenway sees a mix of resident homeless people, joggers and tourists taking in the ocean and pier views. Sunsets are priceless.

🏃 Activities

What's the number-one activity destination in Santa Monica? That would be that loamy, quarter-mile-deep, 5-mile stretch of golden sand lapped by the Pacific. Water temperatures become tolerable by late spring and are highest – about 67°F (20°C) – in September. Water quality varies; for updated conditions check the Beach Report Card (www.healthebay.org).

The waves in Santa Monica are gentle and well shaped for beginner surfers, as well as bodyboarders and bodysurfers. The best swimming beaches are Will Rogers State Beach on the border of Pacific Palisades, and the beach south of the pier.

Annenberg Community Beach House
BEACH

(☑ 310-458-4904; www.annenbergbeachhouse. com; 415 Pacific Coast Hwy; per hour/day Nov-Mar $3/8, Apr-Oct $3/12, pool admission adult/senior/child $10/5/4) Like a fancy beach club for the rest of us, this sleek and attractive city-owned spot, built on actress Marion Davies' estate (she had a thing with William Randolph Hearst), opens to the public on a first-come-first-served basis. It has a lap pool, lounge chairs, yoga classes, beach volleyball, fitness room and art gallery.

Santa Monica Mountains
HIKING

(www.nps.gov/samo/index.htm) A haven for hikers, trekkers and mountain bikers, the northwestern-most stretch of the Santa Monica Mountains is where nature gets bigger and wilder, with jaw-dropping red-rock canyons, and granite outcrops with sublime sea views. The best trails are in Pacific Palisades, Topanga and Malibu.

🛏 Sleeping

Let's face it. Santa Monica is not the place to come for a cheap sleep or a party hotel, but if you want the genuine high-end beach-front experience, it's hard to do better. And, in fact, there are some bargains to be had. At the lowest end, the youth hostel is one of the best we've seen.

HI Los Angeles-Santa Monica
HOSTEL $

(☑ 310-393-9913; www.hilosangeles.org; 1436 2nd St; dm low season $27-45, May-Oct $40-55, r with shared bath $109-140, with private bath $160-230; ⊝❋@☎; M Expo Line to Downtown Santa Monica) Near the beach and Promenade, this hostel has an enviable location and modernized facilities that rival properties charging many times more. Its approximately 275 beds in single-sex dorms are clean and safe, private rooms are decorated with hipster chic, and public spaces (courtyard, library, TV room, dining room, communal kitchen) let you lounge and surf.

Casa del Mar
HOTEL $$$

(☑ 310-581-5533; www.hotelcasadelmar.com; 1910 Ocean Way; r from $525; P⊝❋@☎❄❋) This mid-1920s beachfront building has alluring Spanish-Mediterranean style and 129 rooms and suites in whites and pale blues designed by Michael Smith, who did the Obama family's private residence. Room rates basically

RUNYON CANYON

Slip on your activewear and baseball cap and join the buff and their canine companions on a hike through **Runyon Canyon** (www.runyoncanyonhike.com; 2000 N Fuller Ave; ⊙ dawn-dusk). Sitting at the eastern end of the Santa Monica Mountains, its one-loop track is the city's favorite spot to jog, power walk or simply stroll while chatting contracts, plots or last night's date. Then again, you could just get lost in those commanding city views, or wonder which famous face is hiding behind those over-sized D&G shades. Best of all, it's less than a one-mile walk from Hollywood/Highland station on the Metro Red Line, making it an easy urban escape.

correlate with best views. 'Casa' is most definitely not a thumping pool-party scene, but there is a beach concierge for bikes, blades and umbrellas.

Shutters on the Beach
HOTEL $$$

(☑ 310-458-0030; www.shuttersonthebeach.com; 1 Pico Blvd; r $525; P@☎) Bringing classic Cape Cod charm to the Pacific coast, the 198 rooms here have a beach-cottage feel with marble baths, wood floors, spectacular ocean views and tiny balconies with white-washed shutters. The in-house beach cafe is charming and tasty, and the chichi **One Pico** restaurant draws rave reviews. This is as upscale as Santa Monica nests get.

🍴 Eating

There's good food scattered all around SaMo, particularly on Main St and around Third Street Promenade. You'll also find a sort of gourmet gulch around 10th St and Wilshire Blvd.

Santa Monica Farmers Markets
MARKET $

(www.smgov.net/portals/farmersmarket; Arizona Ave, btwn 2nd & 3rd Sts; ⊙ Arizona Ave 8:30am-1:30pm Wed, 8am-1pm Sat, Main St 8:30am-1:30pm Sun; ❤) 🍴 You haven't really experienced Santa Monica until you've explored one of its weekly outdoor farmers markets stocked with organic fruits, vegetables, flowers, baked goods and freshly shucked oysters. The mack daddy is the Wednesday market, around the intersection of 3rd and Arizona – it's the biggest and arguably the best for fresh produce, and is often patrolled by local chefs.

Huckleberry

CAFE $

(☎310-451-2311; www.huckleberrycafe.com; 1014 Wilshire Blvd; mains $10-14; ⊘8am-5pm) Part of the epicurean family from the couple behind **Rustic Canyon** (☎310-393-7050; www.rusticcanyonwinebar.com; 1119 Wilshire Blvd; dishes $13-40; ⊘5:30-10:30pm Sun-Thu, to 11pm Fri & Sat), **Milo & Olive** (☎310-453-6776; www.miloandolive.com; 2723 Wilshire Blvd; dishes $7-20; ⊘7am-11pm) and Cassia, Huckleberry's Zoe Nathan devises some of the most exquisite pastries in the city: salted caramel bars, crostatas bursting with blueberries, maple bacon biscuits, and pumpkin and ginger tea cakes. A simple fried-egg sandwich goes gourmet with Niman Ranch bacon, Gruyère, arugula and aioli.

Santa Monica Seafood

SEAFOOD $$

(☎310-393-5244; www.santamonicaseafood.com; 1000 Wilshire Blvd; appetizers $7-15, mains $14-30; ⊘9am-9pm Mon-Sat, to 8pm Sun; P ♿) The best seafood market in Southern California offers a tasty oyster bar and market cafe, where you can sample delicious chowder, salmon burgers, albacore melts, oysters on the half shell and pan-roasted cod.

Cassia

SOUTHEAST ASIAN $$$

(☎310-393-6699; 1314 7th St; appetizers $12-24, mains $18-77; ⊘5-10pm Sun-Thu, to 11pm Fri & Sat; P) Ever since it opened in 2015, open, airy Cassia has made about every local and national 'best' list of LA restaurants. Chef Bryant Ng draws on his Chinese-Singaporean heritage in dishes such as *kaya* toast (with coconut jam, butter and a slow-cooked egg), 'sunbathing' prawns, and the encompassing Vietnamese *pot au feu:* short-rib stew, vegetables, bone marrow and delectable accompaniments.

Drinking

Dogtown Coffee

CAFE

(www.dogtowncoffee.com; 2003 Main St; ⊘5:30am-5pm Mon-Fri, from 6:30am Sat & Sun) Set in the old Zephyr surf shop headquarters, where skateboarding was invented during a 1970s drought that emptied pools across LA, it brews great coffee and makes a mean breakfast burrito, the preferred nutritional supplement of surfers the world over. And it's open for dawn patrol.

Bungalow

LOUNGE

(www.thebungalowsm.com; 101 Wilshire Blvd, Fairmont Miramar Hotel; ⊘5pm-2am Mon-Fri, noon-2am Sat, noon-10pm Sun) A Brent Bolthouse nightspot, the indoor-outdoor lounge at the Fairmont Miramar was one of the hottest nights out in LA when it burst onto the scene a couple of years ago. It's since settled down, and like most Westside spots can be too dude-centric late in the evening, but the setting is elegant, and there's still beautiful mischief to be found here.

Chez Jay

BAR

(www.chezjays.com; 1657 Ocean Ave; ⊘11:45am-2pm & 5:30-9:30pm Mon-Fri, 9am-1:45pm & 5:30-9:30pm Sat & Sun) Rocking since 1959, this nautical-themed dive has seen its share of Hollywood intrigue from the Rat Pack to the Brat Pack. To this day it's dark and dank and all the more glorious for it. The classic steak and seafood menu's not bad, either.

☆ Entertainment

Harvelle's

BLUES

(☎310-395-1676; www.harvelles.com; 1432 4th St; cover $5-15) This dark blues grotto has been packing 'em in since 1931, but somehow still manages to feel like a well-kept secret. There are no big-name acts here, but the quality is usually high. Sunday's Toledo Show mixes soul, jazz and cabaret, and Wednesday night brings the always-funky House of Vibe All-Stars.

Twilight Concert Series

LIVE MUSIC

(www.santamonicapier.org/twilight; ⊘7-10pm Thu Jul-early Sep) FREE This beloved local institution brings Santa Monicans of all stripes to rock out by the thousands on the pier and on the sand below, gigging local to world-famous names, including Mavis Staples, Save Ferris and the Psychedelic Furs.

Aero Theater

CINEMA

(www.americancinematheque.com; 1328 Montana Ave) Santa Monica's original movie theater (c 1940) is now operated by **American Cinematheque** (Map p98; ☎323-461-2020; www.egyptiantheatre.com; 6712 Hollywood Blvd; Ⓜ Red Line to Hollywood/Highland), where it screens old and neo classics, and offers Q&A sessions with bigwigs from time to time. Check its online calendar for upcoming shows.

Shopping

Puzzle Zoo

GAMES

(☎310-393-9201; www.puzzlezoo.com; 1411 Third St Promenade; ⊘10am-10pm Sun-Thu, to 11pm Fri & Sat; ♿) Those searching galaxy-wide for the caped Lando Calrissian action figure, look no more. Puzzle Zoo stocks every imaginable *Star Wars* or anime figurine this

Santa Monica State Beach (p115)

side of Endor. There's also an encyclopedic selection of puzzles, board games and toys. Kids adore it.

🛈 Information

Santa Monica Information Kiosk (1400 Ocean Ave; ◎9am-5pm Jun-Aug, 10am-4pm Sep-May)

🛈 Getting Around

Santa Monica's **Big Blue Bus** (☑310-451-5444; www.bigbluebus.com) serves routes throughout the city and beyond. However, the most Santa Monica way to get around these days is by bi-

cycle. Many outlets rent by the hour or day, including the city-run **Santa Monica Bike Center** (☑310-656-8500; www.smbikecenter.com; 1555 2nd St; bikes per 2hr/day from $20/30; ◎7am-8pm Mon-Fri, from 8am Sat & Sun; Ⓜ Expo Line to Downtown Santa Monica) and the beachside **Perry's Café** (☑310-939-0000; www.perryscafe.com; Ocean Front Walk; bikes per hour/day from $10/30, boogie boards $7/20; ◎9am-7:30pm Mon-Fri, from 8:30am Sat & Sun). For shorter trips, Santa Monica also operates its **bike share program** (www.santamonicabikeshare.com; per hour $7, monthly/annually $25/99), where you pick up bikes at kiosks and return them at other kiosks.

USA Driving Guide

With a comprehensive network of interstate highways, enthusiastic car culture and jaw-dropping scenery, the USA is an ideal road-tripping destination.

Fast Facts: Driving

Right or left? Drive on the right

Manual or automatic? Most rental agencies offer both

Blood alcohol concentration limit 0.08%

Top speed limit 75mph (on some interstate highways)

DRIVER'S LICENSE

Foreign visitors can legally drive a car in the USA for up to 12 months using their home driver's license. However, an International Driving Permit (IDP) will have more credibility with US traffic police, especially if your home license doesn't have a photo or isn't in English. Your automobile association at home can issue an IDP, valid for one year, for a small fee. Always carry your home license together with the IDP.

To ride a motorcycle in the USA, you will need either a valid US state motorcycle license or an IDP specially endorsed for motorcycles.

INSURANCE

Don't put the key into the ignition if you don't have insurance, which is legally required. You risk financial ruin and legal consequences if there's an accident. If you already have auto insurance, or if you buy travel insurance that covers car rentals, make sure your policy has adequate liability coverage for where you will be driving, as different states specify different minimum levels of coverage.

Car-rental companies will provide liability insurance, but most charge extra. Rental companies almost never include collision-damage insurance for the vehicle. Instead, they offer an optional Collision Damage Waiver (CDW) or Loss Damage Waiver (LDW), usually with an initial deductible cost of between $100 and $500. For an extra premium, you can usually get this deductible covered as well. Paying extra for some or all of this insurance increases the cost of a rental car by as much as $30 a day.

Many credit cards offer free collision damage coverage for rental cars if you rent for 15 days or less and charge the total rental to your card. This is a good way to avoid paying extra fees to the rental company, but note that if there's an accident, sometimes you must pay the car-rental company first and then seek reimbursement from the credit-card company. There may be exceptions that are not covered too, such as 'exotic' rentals (eg 4WD Jeeps or convertibles). Check your credit-card policy.

Driving Problem-Buster

What should I do if my car breaks down? Call the roadside emergency assistance number of your car-rental company or, if you're driving your own vehicle, your automobile club. Otherwise, call information (☑411) for the number of the nearest towing service or auto-repair shop.

What if I'm involved in an accident? If it's safe to do so, pull over to the side of the road. For minor 'fender benders' with no injuries or significant property damage, exchange insurance and driver's license information with other drivers and file a report with your car-rental company or insurance provider as soon as possible. For major accidents, call ☑911 and wait for the police and emergency services to arrive.

What if I'm stopped by the police or California Highway Patrol? Don't get out of the car unless asked. Be courteous and keep your hands where the officer can see them at all times (eg on the steering wheel). For traffic violations, there's typically a 30-day period in which to pay a fine online or by mail. Police can legally give roadside sobriety checks to assess if you've been drinking or using drugs.

What should I do if my car gets towed? Call the local police department's non-emergency number and ask where to pick up your car. Do this immediately, since towing and storage fees can quickly amount to hundreds of dollars.

RENTING A VEHICLE

Cars

Car rental is a competitive business in the USA. Most rental companies require that you have a major credit card, be at least 25 years old and have a valid driver's license. Some major national companies may rent to drivers between the ages of 21 and 24 for an additional charge of around $25 per day. Those under 21 years are usually not permitted to rent at all.

Car-rental prices vary wildly, so shop around. The average daily rate for a small car ranges from around $20 to $75, or $125 to $500 per week. If you belong to an auto club or frequent-flier program, you may get a discount (or earn rewards points or miles).

Some other things to keep in mind: most national agencies make 'unlimited mileage' standard on all cars, but independents might charge extra for this. Tax on car rental varies by state and agency location; always ask for the total cost *including* all taxes and fees. Most agencies charge more if you pick the car up in one place and drop it off in another, and usually only national agencies offer this option. Be careful about adding extra days or turning in a car early – extra days may be charged at a premium rate, or an early return may jeopardize any weekly or monthly discounts you originally arranged.

Some major national companies, including Avis, Budget and Hertz, offer 'green' fleets of hybrid rental cars (eg Toyota Priuses and Honda Civics), though you'll usually have to pay quite a bit more to rent a hybrid. Some independent local agencies, especially on the West Coast, also offer hybrid-vehicle rentals. Try Southern California's **Simply RAC** (www.simplyrac.com) and Hawaii's **Bio-Beetle** (www.bio-beetle.com).

Motorcycles & RVs

If you dream of cruising across America on a Harley, **EagleRider** (www.eaglerider.com) rents motorcycles in major cities nationwide. If a recreational vehicle (RV) is more your style, places such as www.usarvrentals.com and www.cruiseamerica.com can help. Beware that rental and insurance fees for these vehicles are expensive.

MAPS

Tourist information offices and visitor centers distribute free but often very basic maps. GPS navigation can't be relied upon everywhere, notably in thick forests and remote areas. If you're planning on doing a lot of driving, you may want a more detailed fold-out road map or map atlas, such as those published by Rand McNally

Road-Trip Resources

AUTO CLUBS

American Automobile Association (AAA; ☑800-874-7532, towing, roadside assistance 800-222-4357; www.aaa.com) Offers maps and roadside assistance for members.

Better World Club (☑866-238-1137; www.betterworldclub.com) Ecofriendly auto club that supports environmental causes and offers add-on or stand-alone emergency roadside assistance for cyclists, too. An annual membership costs from $40 for cyclists and $59 for drivers.

MAPS

America's Byways (http://byways.org) Inspiring itineraries, maps and directions for scenic drives.

Google Maps (http://maps.google.com) Turn-by-turn driving directions with estimated traffic delays.

ROAD CONDITIONS & CLOSURES

US Department of Transportation (www.fhwa.dot.gov/trafficinfo) Links to state and local road conditions, traffic and weather.

(www.randmcnally.com). Members of the American Automobile Association (AAA) and its international auto-club affiliates (bring your membership card from home) can pick up free maps at AAA branch offices nationwide.

ROAD CONDITIONS & HAZARDS

America's highways are thought of as legendary ribbons of unblemished asphalt, but that's not always the case. Road hazards include potholes, city commuter traffic, wandering wildlife and cell-phone-wielding, kid-distracted and enraged drivers. Caution, foresight, courtesy and luck usually gets you past them. For nationwide traffic and road-closure information, click to www.fhwa.dot.gov/trafficinfo.

In places where winter driving is an issue, many cars are fitted with steel-studded snow tires, while snow chains can sometimes be required in mountain areas. Driving off-road, or on dirt roads, is often forbidden by car-rental companies, and it can be very dangerous in wet weather.

In deserts and range country, livestock sometimes graze next to unfenced roads. These areas are signed as 'Open Range' or with the silhouette of a steer. Where deer and other wild animals frequently appear roadside, you'll see signs with the silhouette of a leaping deer. Take these signs seriously, particularly at dusk and dawn.

ROAD RULES

In the USA, cars drive on the right-hand side of the road. The use of seat belts is required in every state except New Hampshire, and child safety seats are required in every state. Most car-rental agencies rent child safety seats for $10 to $14 per day, but you must reserve them when booking. In some states, motorcyclists are required to wear helmets.

On interstate highways, the speed limit is sometimes raised to 75mph. Unless otherwise posted, the speed limit is generally 55mph or 65mph on highways, 25mph to 35mph in cities and towns, and as low as 15mph in school zones (strictly enforced during school hours). It's forbidden to pass a school bus when its lights are flashing.

Unless signs prohibit it, you may turn right at a red light after first coming to a full stop – note that turning right on red is illegal in NYC. At four-way stop signs, cars should proceed in order of arrival; when two cars arrive simultaneously, the one on the right has the right of way. When in doubt, just politely wave the other driver ahead. When emergency vehicles (ie police, fire or ambulance) approach from either direction, pull over safely and get out of the way.

In many states, it's illegal to talk on a handheld cell phone while driving; use a hands-free device instead.

The maximum legal blood-alcohol concentration for drivers is 0.08%. Penalties are very severe for 'DUI' – driving under the influence of alcohol and/or drugs. Police can give roadside sobriety checks to assess if you've been drinking or using drugs. If you fail, they'll require you to take a breath test, urine test or blood test to determine the level of alcohol or drugs in your body. Refusing to be tested is treated the same as if you'd taken the test and failed.

In some states it's illegal to carry 'open containers' of alcohol in a vehicle, even if they're empty.

PARKING

➡ Parking is usually plentiful and free in small towns and rural areas, but often scarce and/or expensive in cities.

➡ When parking on the street, read all posted regulations and restrictions (eg street-cleaning hours and permit-only residential areas) and pay attention to colored curbs, or you may be ticketed and towed.

➡ You can pay municipal parking meters and sidewalk pay stations with coins (eg quarters) and sometimes credit or debit cards.

➡ Expect to pay $30 to $50 for overnight parking in a city lot or garage.

➡ Flat-fee valet parking at hotels, restaurants, nightclubs etc is common in major cities, especially Los Angeles.

FUEL

Many gas stations in the USA have fuel pumps with automated credit-card pay screens. Some machines ask for your ZIP code after you swipe your card. For foreign travelers, or those with cards issued outside the US, you'll have to pay inside before fueling up. Just indicate how much you'd like to put on the card. If there's still credit left over after you fuel up, pop back inside and the attendant will put the difference back on your card.

SAFETY

Vehicle theft, break-ins and vandalism are a problem mostly in urban areas. Be sure to lock your vehicle's doors, leave the windows rolled up and use any anti-theft devices that have been installed (eg car alarm, steering-wheel lock). Do not leave any valuables visible inside your vehicle; instead, stow them in the trunk before arriving at your destination, or else take them with you once you've parked.

USA Playlist

'(Get Your Kicks on) Route 66' Bobby Troup, as recorded by Nat King Cole

'I've Been Everywhere' Johnny Cash

'This Land Is Your Land' Woody Guthrie

'Born to Be Wild' Steppenwolf

'Fast Car' Tracy Chapman

'Runnin' Down a Dream' Tom Petty & the Heartbreakers

'Life Is a Highway' Tom Cochrane

BEHIND THE SCENES

ACKNOWLEDGMENTS

Climate map data adapted from Peel MC, Finlayson BL & McMahon TA (2007) 'Updated World Map of the Köppen-Geiger Climate Classification', *Hydrology and Earth System Sciences*, 11, 163-344.

Cover photograph: Route 66 from above, California, Cavan Images/Getty Images ©.

HOLLYWOOD ™ & Design © 2018 Hollywood Chamber of Commerce. The Hollywood Sign is a trademark and intellectual property of the Hollywood Chamber of Commerce. All Rights Reserved.

THIS BOOK

This 3rd edition of *Route 66 Road Trips* was researched and written by Andrew Bender, Cristian Bonetto, Mark Johanson, Hugh McNaughtan, Christopher Pitts, Ryan Ver Berkmoes and Karla Zimmerman. The 1st edition was written by Karla Zimmerman, Amy Balfour and Nate Cavalieri. This guidebook was produced by the following:

Curator Kate Mathews

Destination Editors Alex Howard, Trisha Ping, Sarah Stocking, Angela Tinson

Product Editors Elizabeth Jones, Lauren O'Connell

Senior Cartographers Alison Lyall, Julie Sheridan

Book Designers Nicholas Colicchia, Nicolas d'Hoedt

Assisting Editors Pete Cruttenden, Clare Healey, Gabrielle Stefanos

Cover Researcher Fergal Condon

Thanks to Marzia Ciurca, Grace Dobell, James Hardy, Karen Henderson, Sonia Kapoor, Indra Kilfoyle, Alison Killilea, Catherine Naghten, Kirsten Rawlings, Wibowo Rusli, Lyahna Spencer, Angela Tinson, Bill Wallace

OUR STORY

A beat-up old car, a few dollars in the pocket and a sense of adventure. In 1972 that's all Tony and Maureen Wheeler needed for the trip of a lifetime – across Europe and Asia overland to Australia. It took several months, and at the end – broke but inspired – they sat at their kitchen table writing and stapling together their first travel guide, *Across Asia on the Cheap*. Within a week they'd sold 1500 copies. Lonely Planet was born.

Today, Lonely Planet has offices in the US, Ireland and China, with a network of more than 2000 contributors in every corner of the globe. We share Tony's belief that 'a great guidebook should do three things: inform, educate and amuse'.

INDEX

OUR WRITERS

ANDREW BENDER

Award-winning travel and food writer Andrew Bender has written three dozen Lonely Planet guidebooks (from *Amsterdam* to *Los Angeles*, *Germany* to *USA* and over a dozen titles about Japan), plus numerous articles for lonelyplanet.com. A native New Englander, he now lives in the Los Angeles area.

CRISTIAN BONETTO

Cristian has contributed to over 30 Lonely Planet guides to date, including *New York City*, *Italy*, *Venice & the Veneto*, *Naples & the Amalfi Coast*, *Denmark*, *Copenhagen*, *Sweden* and *Singapore*. When not on the road, you'll find him slurping espresso in his beloved hometown, Melbourne. Instagram: rexcat75.

MARK JOHANSON

Mark Johanson's travel-writing career began as something of a quarter-life crisis, and he's happily spent the past eight years circling the globe reporting for Australian travel magazines, British newspapers, American lifestyles and global media outlets. When not on the road, you'll find him gazing at the Andes from his home in Santiago, Chile. Follow the adventure at www.markjohanson.com

HUGH MCNAUGHTAN

A former English lecturer, Hugh swapped grant applications for visa applications, and turned his love of travel into a full-time thing. He's never happier than when on the road with his two daughters. Except perhaps on the cricket field...

CHRISTOPHER PITTS

Infinitely curious about the other side of the world, Chris left the US to study Chinese in university, living for several years in Kunming and Shanghai. A chance encounter in an elevator led to a Paris relocation, where he lived with his wife and two children for over a decade before the lure of Colorado's sunny skies and outdoor adventure proved too great to resist.

RYAN VER BERKMOES

Ryan Ver Berkmoes has written more than 110 guidebooks for Lonely Planet. Since college he has been traveling the world, both for pleasure and for work – which are often indistinguishable. Ryan calls New York City home. Read more at ryanverberkmoes. com and at @ryanvb.

KARLA ZIMMERMAN

Karla lives in Chicago, where she eat doughnuts, yells at the Cubs, and writes stuff for books, magazines and websites when she's not doing the first two things. She has contributed to 40-plus guidebooks and travel anthologies covering destinations in Europe, Asia, Africa, North America and the Caribbean. To learn more, follow her on Instagram and Twitter (@karlazimmerman).

Contributing Writers: Sara Benson, Gregor Clark, Andrea Schulte-Peevers

Published by Lonely Planet Global Limited
CRN 554153
3rd edition – Oct 2022
ISBN 978 1 78701 637 8
© Lonely Planet 2022   Photographs © as indicated 2022
10 9 8 7 6 5 4 3 2 1
Printed in China

Although the authors and Lonely Planet have taken all reasonable care in preparing this book, we make no warranty about the accuracy or completeness of its content and, to the maximum extent permitted, disclaim all liability arising from its use.